WYE IN
EIGHTEENTH CENTURY

by

Bryan Keith-Lucas

a sequel to
'The Old Book of Wye'
by G. E. Hubbard

1

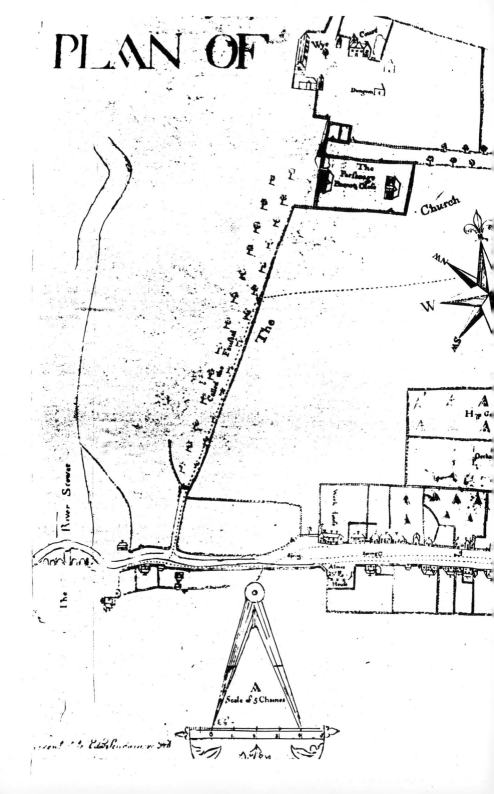

PLAN OF

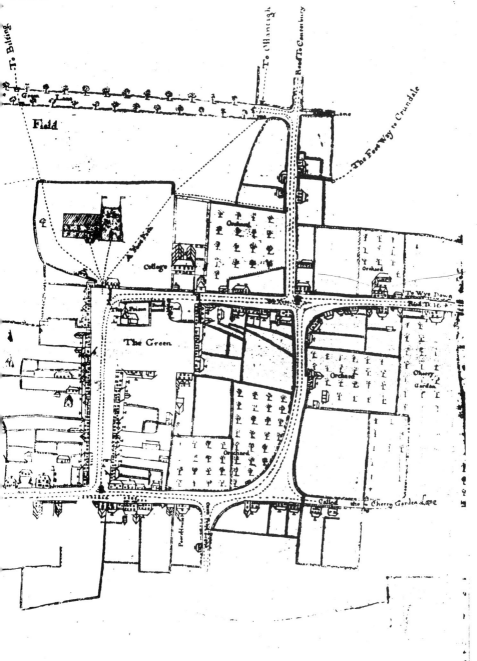

E TOWN 1746

WYE IN THE 18th CENTURY

by

Bryan Keith-Lucas

My thanks are due to Wye Parish Council, the owner of the parochial records on which this account is based, and to the Librarian of Wye College, in whose safe custody they are kept.

A number of the volumes in this collection are two or three hundred years old, and have inevitably become somewhat worn and tattered. Messrs Alexander and Alexander (UK) Ltd. generously financed the rebinding of the volumes in vellum to survive for centuries to come, and also made a most welcome contribution toward the cost of publication.

I am grateful also to Brian Grantley-Smith, the Chairman of the Wye Historical Society, and to Joanna Pazowski, who have spent many hours deciphering and transcribing my muddled script.

Contents

To Mr Knowles

To Boucrets Heirs

To Crophot

To The Earle of Winchilsea

Winchilsea

To Mr Elden

Lands Belonging to Mr Knight

To
the
Earle
of Winchilsea

Wood Land Belonging To Mr Carl Curteis

Goudley Heirs

To Search

To Mr Clement Heirs

To Harman's Heirs

Mr Crofts

A Map & Description
of A Wood Called Kings
Wood Being in the Parish of Wye in
the County of Kent Belonging to the Right
Honourable The Earle of Winchilsea & Nottingham
With the whole Content of the Wood and Parcels Adjoyn
ing to it See the Table And shewing the Common High
Roads & Throwes or by the Said Wood, with the Gates
the Pound, the Pains and Pounds Likewise of those
Persons Land Lyes in and whose Bounds to the Said
wood, it Being Accuratly Taken From the Yearly
Plans when Felld Beginning From the Year 1739
And Ended this Year 1762 which forms this Map
Measured and Mape By the Order of the
Above Said Noble Earle By
Michael Mann Surveyer in
Wye

KINGS

WOO

To Mr Knowles

To John Sawbridge Esq

To Mr Midwill

To Mr Skins

To Sr John Sawbridge Esq

To Cook Esq

To Sr John Filmor Bar

To John Sawbridge Esq

To John Sawbridge Esq

To Lady Guildford

To Cook Esq

To Searle Goudleys Heirs

Wood

Land

Belonging

To

Lings

Guildford

A Scale of 20 Chains

To Thomas Knight

Map of King's Wood by
Michael Moon, 1762, show-
ing the land given to the poor
of Wye by Richard Driland.
Reproduced by permission
of the Trustees of the
Winchilsea Settled Estates.

Introduction

In 1951 my uncle, Ernest Hubbard, published his admirable book, *The Old Book of Wye*, based on the volume of Churchwardens' accounts covering the years between 1515 and 1663, which had been found after being lost for many years.

In addition to that volume the Parish Council has a considerable number of parochial records. These include the Churchwardens' Accounts from 1663 to 1819 (four volumes), the Overseers' Accounts from 1663 to 1819 (Poor Books, twelve volumes), the Vestry Minutes from 1724 to 1851 and 1881 to 1947 (four volumes), and a number of other books and bundles of documents referring to the affairs of Wye in the 18th and 19th centuries. All these are housed in the Library of Wye College.

In 1854 a list was made of the parish records in the Church Vestry. It was a valuable list of a number of valuable documents, but, according to a note made at the time

> "the undermentioned documents were destroyed as useless
> Old Workhouse Account Books
> Old Highway Account Books
> Miscellaneous old papers, etc."

About a hundred years later Ernest Hubbard checked the list again and found that a few more volumes were missing, including "a Book called Lady Joanna Thornhill's Charity from 1727 to 1818". None the less there remain today enough to enable us to get a picture of Wye as it was two or three hundred years ago.

This essay is essentially an account of the contents of these volumes, in so far as they illustrate the way that Wye was governed in the 18th century. It does not purport to be a history of Wye, nor does it deal with aspects of the government of Wye which are not related to the content of these volumes; Quarter Sessions and Petty Sessions, the Courts Leet and the Courts Baron, the work of the Constables and the Turnpike Trusts all lie beyond the scope of the present work.

In the 18th century Wye was a quiet and ordinary place. Charles Seymour, who described himself as a "Teacher of the Classics, etc. at Canterbury" in his *New Topographical, Historical and Commercial Survey of the Cities, Towns and Villages of the County of Kent*, published in 1776, describes it as "a poor deserted place", and said that it "has a bridge over the Stour and a harbour for barges." Edward Wedlake Brayley in his *Beauties of England and Wales*, published in 1808, stated that "Wye, called by Leland 'a pratie market townlet' is now only a considerable village, the market having been long disused." Edward Hasted, writing in the late eighteenth century, said that

> The town, which stands low and damp and from that and its soil an unpleasant situation, is a neat well built town, consisting of two parallel and two cross streets, the whole unpaved. There is a large green in it, built round, on one side of which is the church and college close to it, and on the other a house which was once the gaol to the manor-court, but long since disused.

At the end of the century the population was about 1200.

Wye was in the seventeenth and early eighteenth century a strongly Royalist village, with a continuing adherence to the old (or Roman) faith. Among the leading figures was the Rev. Thomas Brett, who refused to take the oath of allegiance to the Hanoverian kings, and left the Church of England, becoming a Non-juror bishop. His son, Nicholas, was chaplain to Sir Robert Cotton, a Jacobite exile in France. Richard Thornhill, the husband of Lady Joanna Thornhill who founded the school, enlisted a troop of horse to support the King when he raised his standard at Nottingham in 1639. The charity founded by Robert Cole was a blatant declaration of opposition to Cromwell and to the execution of Charles the First. A number of leading inhabitants including Sir Thomas Kemp, Richard Dryland and Robert Searles were accused of supporting the Catholic faith.[1]

There was little change in the pattern of local administration throughout the century. It was a very stable period, unlike the 17th century with the Civil War, the Protectorate and the ejection of the Stuarts, and unlike the 19th century, with the creation of the Poor Law Unions, Guardians, County Councils, District and Parish Councils. The main developments in rural local government in the 18th century were the establishment of turnpike trusts, and the development of the Poor Law towards the workhouses and unions of parishes. In Wye the pattern was much the same in 1800 as it had been in 1700.

---

[1] See Hubbard, *Old Book of Wye*, pp. 17-49, 144-146 and Nigel Washington-Jones, article in *Wye Local History*, Spring 1994, *Wye and the King over the Water*.

There was in the 18th century no central authority to supervise the working of local government from Whitehall. If one parish developed a pattern of government different from that of other parishes there was nobody whose job it was to make them comply with the national pattern. In the course of the eighteenth century 85 Acts of Parliament relating to the Poor Law were passed, but there was nobody whose duty it was to see that they were enforced. In 1697 an Act had been passed making it compulsory for all people in receipt of relief to wear badges on their right sleeves. It does not appear that this was rigidly enforced in Wye, but in 1725 there is an entry in the Overseers Accounts of -

> Pd for a warr; to make the Poor were the Badges 1/0d

Whether or not they did so is not recorded, but there is no further mention of the matter.

The manorial courts were regularly held, on behalf of the Lords of the Manor, the Earls of Winchilsea. They had, however, become little more than formalities. The Homage of the Manor was represented by two freemen of the manor,[1] who presented the various sales and inheritances of land in the manor, for which modest reliefs (i.e. payments) were due to the Lord of the Manor. These were duly recorded in imposing vellum volumes, but the total income can scarcely have paid for the steward's fees. The Court of Record which had previously sat on every Monday three weeks, no longer assembled, and the minor manors referred to in Morris's History of Wye - Aldons, (alias Perry), Fannescombe, Fanneswood, Hinxell and Raymonds - seem to have faded out by the eighteenth century, though the Wye Overseers continued to pay 2/9d a year for quitrent to the Manor of Perry.

In the 18th Century Wye Court was a substantial sized house, the home of the principal farmer of the parish. But according to Furley[2] Edward I and his retinue were generously entertained there in 1299, and Edward II "with a great train of household" kept Christmas there. From this it seems that Wye Court had once been a very much larger building. This would have included the dungeon or "Lollards Hole" which was filled in early in the 19th century.

---

[1] Valentine Austen and Thomas Quested were commonly members of the "Homage" (i.e. The assembly of tenants of the Manor). Quested served also as Constable of the Upper Half Hundred of Wye (an officer of the Quarter Sessions)

[2] Robert Furley, A History of the Weald of Kent (1874) Vol II, pp. 253,266

The government of Wye, as of nearly all the other villages of England, was vested in the parish assembly known as the vestry, so called from the custom of meeting in the vestry of the parish church. These vestry meetings were not established by any Act of Parliament or other legal authority, and no rules existed to define who were entitled to attend the meetings, who should preside, or what their powers were.

From the days of the Restoration these meetings of the parishioners became increasingly formalised, though never defined in statute law. It came to be accepted that the chair should be taken by the Vicar or Rector, even if the Squire or the Lord of the Manor was there. In some parishes a small inner group or caucus took control of the vestry and in many cases abused their authority, becoming increasingly corrupt. So widespread were these abuses that in 1693 Sir John Guise introduced a Bill into the House of Commons to regulate these "select vestries". This bill, and several others like it in subsequent years, was not passed, but since 1698 a similar bill has been introduced in the House of Lords at the beginning of every session. It never gets beyond the "first reading" and survives only as a formal claim that the redress of grievances must come before the House will deal with the Government's business. There have, in fact, been no select vestries in the country for a century or more.

In Wye there was not a "select vestry", but on the other hand it was not a truly "open vestry", in that the records show that there were rarely more than a dozen people at the meetings,[1] and these included the curate (Wye did not have a vicar or rector, but only a perpetual curate), who usually took the chair, the overseers of the poor, two churchwardens and half a dozen other substantial farmers and tradesmen.

In many parishes the vestry used to meet first in the church as a matter of form, and then adjourn to the inn, where they drank beer at the expense of the parish rates, and discussed the problems of the village. In Wye, however, the meetings appear always to have been held in the church, without adjournment, but some informal meetings were held at the Flying Horse or occasionally at the King's Head.

There being no statutory definition of the powers of the vestry, and the legal doctrine of *ultra vires*[2] not yet having been conceived, the vestry did

---

[1] The Poor Book shows that at one meeting in 1702 there were fifty people present, but no explanation is given for this large attendance. There was a select vestry in Wye in 1826 and 1827, but it does not appear to have continued beyond those years.

[2] The principle that a statutory body can legally only do such things as are authorised by statute.

whatever its members thought to be necessary. It not only appointed the parish officers - overseers of the poor and church wardens, masters of the workhouse, managers of the "Pesthouse", sextons and others - but it came, more and more, to give them orders; to treat them as if they were employ-ees of the vestry, or local government officers under a local authority, rather than as independent officers.

The Overseers of the Poor

The Elizabethan Poor Law Act of 1601 (43 Eliz. c.2) provided that:-

> "The Churchwardens of every parish and four, three or two substantial householders there . . . to be nominated yearly in Easter Week or within one month after Easter, under the hand and seal of two or more Justices of the Peace in the same county, whereof one to be of the quorum,[1] dwelling in or near the parish or division, shall be called Overseers of the Poor for the same parish".

There is no mention here of the vestry, but as in other parishes, it was the vestry in Wye that actually chose the overseers. The Justices of the Peace then certified the vestry's choice by signing the document. The office of overseer was not popular, it involved much work, and it tended to make the officers unpopular with their fellow parishioners. Their power over the people of the village was very great. To the poor people of the parish it mattered more who was the parish overseer than who was in office in distant Westminster.

The Poor Law Act of 1601 had prescribed the duties of the overseers: they were to administer the poor law, and, subject to confirmation by the magistrates, to raise a rate, or "sess", for that purpose. They were to be responsible for the poor of their own village, with no clear duty towards others. They were unpaid, and served for only a single year at a time. Though in Wye they were usually literate, occasionally someone was appointed who could only sign his name by making his mark, and most of them were insufficiently experienced to be able to keep complicated accounts. In practice most of the clerical work was done by the vestry clerk, who often was the village schoolmaster or, later in the century, a local solicitor. By the latter part of the century there appears a "Deputy Overseer", who served for a number of years, and received a salary.

The unpaid overseers did however cover their expenses. There are often such records as "spent at the King's Head at passing the last

---

[1] The Commission of the Peace, appointing the Justices, included a list of senior members of whom (Quorum) one at least should be included in the Bench. Not much attention, apparently, was paid to this in the 18th century.

accounts, 6/-". "Myself and Horse to Canterbury, 4/6d"., or "Expenses signing the Book, 6/6d".

Twice a year the overseers recorded in the "Poor Book" the amount in the pound which was to be levied on all the occupiers of land or houses in the parish (except those in receipt of parochial relief) for the coming six months. Then would come a detailed alphabetical schedule of all the occupiers, and the sess of how much they would each have to contribute for the relief of the poor.

It appears that there was sometimes some difficulty in getting the money out of some of the parishioners, or of the occupiers of land in the parish who did not themselves live in the village (referred to as 'Outdwellers').

In 1736 there is an entry:-

> Pd. Thomas Thatcher Eleven Shillings a Sess he could not get out of the old Countess of Winchilsea.

One reluctant payer was Searles Goatley of Molash who was liable for the sess on parts of King's Wood which he occupied. In July 1742 the vestry resolved that

> John Attwood, Thomas Franklyn, Churchwardens, William Kennett and Tho. Hudson, Overseers, should be indemnified and saved harmless from all charges arising upon account of a sute or any troubles about the getting of Mr Goatley's Sess for his woodland being assessed at one pound a year.

The next entry in the Vestry Minute Book records that

> It is agreed that Searles Goatley Esqr shall be presented to the Ecclesiasticall Court for refusing to pay his Church Sess for woodland lying in the Parish of Wye, which is assessed at one pound a year and with all arrears due amounting to the sum of £1/3/11d as appears in the Church Book.

But in the following year the matter was further complicated by the death of Mr. Goatley, and the churchwardens recorded in their accounts

> Pd. on Esquire Goatley's affair by Vestry Order about the Woodland though the cause was carried on tho' dead in his house at the time of the Sessions by Esquire Robertson's Son of Horton and some of Goatley's Executers . . . 7/6d

Despite this, the churchwardens were unable to get the sesses out of Goatley's heirs for many years to come.

As the sess was levied on the occupier, not the owner, of the land the largest sums were collected from the farmers. Thus William Kennett of Wye Court (then called Court Lodge) had to pay £16/9/3d for the second half year in 1727, while the much wealthier Jacob Sawbridge of Olantigh paid only £1/19/9d. (Though by the end of the century his grandson was paying £39/3/0d).

The modern pattern of investing in Government Stock or company shares had yet to develop, so the principal means of investment was the purchase of land. Thus much of the land was owned by the well-to-do squires of the neighbouring villages. In 1730 these included Sir Wyndham Knatchbull of Mersham, Lord Winchilsea (Lord of the Manor of Wye), Mr Thomas Brodnax-May of Godmersham, Sir Edward Filmer of East Sutton and Sir William Honywood of Evington.

The assessment had by law to be "allowed" by two Justices of the Peace, for which purpose one of the overseers would take the document to the next sitting of Petty Sessions in Ashford. There he would get the signature of two of the Justices - usually the neighbouring squires. But sometimes it appears that the overseer forgot to go to the Petty Sessions, and so the assessment remained unconfirmed. But this made no difference.

The expenditure was recorded in the Overseer's Accounts. These were usually transcribed by the parish clerk in his very legible hand. First came the "Weekly Collections" - the list of parishioners in receipt of regular pensions. The usual allowance of one shilling a week was paid to some thirty people, most of whom were widows, and some of whom lived in neighbouring villages. After this came the list of those whose rent was paid by the overseers out of the poor sess, and then the "Disbursements Extraordinary", which included any other money spent by the overseers. Here the most usual sort of entry is

Let Goodwife Leggett have in want	5/-

But there were many other entries showing how carefully the overseers looked after the poor in the parish. In 1709, for example, these include references to a poor boy, Thomas Dean, who was housed and looked after by the principal farmer of the parish, William Kennett of Wye Court, and to the Pollard brothers, also poor boys supported by the parish.

Wm. Kennett for Dean	£1/6/0d
Pd. for making shirts for Dean and Pollard	2/0d
Spent for a hat for Thomas Dean	1/8d
Pd. Diamond who was behind with his sess	6/0d
Pd. for mending shoes for the Pollards	1/8d
Gave a man with pass[1]	6d

[1] A stranger with a certificate to enable him to travel without being removed back to the parish of his settlement. See page 21.

For Bread and Beer for Thos. Agar	14/4d
For a Coat, Waistcoat, Breetches for Young Boskin	16/0d
Let Thos Argar have in want	2/0d
For mending his shoes	2/0d
A pair of breeches for Dean	2/0d
Valentine Austen for a bed for Goodwife Hame	£1/0/0d
Gave a travelling woman ready to lie in	£1/0/0d
Pd. Mr. Dan for a Certificate for the Canterbury Wench	£1/0/0d
Pd. Goodwife Tong for the Canterbury Wench	2/6d
Spent on Thomas Argars Funeral at Mrs. Boyses	7/6d

Sometimes there are enigmatic entries; in 1726 for example there are several unexplained records -

Gave to a certain body for Secret Service	2/0d
Given to a certain woman, etc	3/0d
Gave Certain Person	1/0d
My expenses going to Ashford with the Loose Fellows[1]	5/0d
Gave Goodman Skilton when he came with a Pretence that my Lord Dunbarton would get him into Chelsea Hospital	5/0d

So also there are some entries which are somewhat cryptic -

Gave Smith more 6d more Shaving & a Wig 15d	1/9d
Pd Wm Bodkin for the Wench that lived at Thatchers laying in there, Dragoon etc[2]	2/0d
Gave the Creature at Bodkins	2/0d

From 1735 to 1737 there are several entries relating to a poor man, Matthew Court, of whom it is recorded that -

Pd Mr Geo Back for the hopp bagg for Matt Courts bed	2/6d
Pd for shaving him and a faggot to help purge him by fire of his lice.	8d

In 1735 Michael Moon, the surveyor, or his father the shoemaker, also helped:

Pd Mich. Moon curing Matt Court of the Itch[3]	5/0d

Other exceptional entries of the same time include

Pd Law. Austen for Mary Pays sitting by his fire the 1/2 year	3/6d
Spent giving away Esquire Sawbridge's beef at Christmas[4]	3/6d

---

[1] Possibly from the village of Loose near Maidstone.

[2] In the following year is an entry - Thomazin and her young Dragoon, 25 weeks - £1/17/6d, and in 1746 there is a note - gave Fairbruce the Dragoon by Vestry order 5/0d. Dragoons were sometimes quartered at Ashford.

[3] Similar entries, referring to other parishioners, appear from time to time.

[4] John Sawbridge of Olantigh gave meat every Christmas to the poor of Wye, to be distributed by the overseers.

Gave the old Scotchman as I suppose in illness	1/0d
Pd for a Load of Straw yts at ye other side	0/0d

Some years later there are further unexplained entries in the Poor Book, such as -

Pd for a letter from Dover & Allowance for ye Fish	1/7d
A horse & expenses to Dover about ye Fish etc.	8/6d
Mr Upperton fetching the Fish home	£1/7/0d

The law of settlement was of Byzantine complexity[1] but essentially it was based on the principle that every parish was responsible for its own poor; that is, the poor people who had a "settlement" there. Thus if a man with a settlement in Wye left the parish and lived elsewhere, he and his wife and children were still the responsibility of Wye. If he fell sick, or grew old, or was unemployed, or his family needed assistance, the Wye overseers were still responsible, and had to pay for his needs and those of his family, either directly or by reimbursing the overseers of the parish where he was living, if they had helped him.

On the other hand he might acquire a new settlement in the parish to which he had moved. This could be done in a variety of ways - by paying the rates in the new parish, by serving as an apprentice there, by occupying a house worth £10 per annum for twelve months, by serving in a parish office as overseer or churchwarden, and in a number of other ways. But the parishes were naturally reluctant to accept labourers or other poor people from other parishes, lest they or their families acquired a settlement there, and then became a financial burden. So, if people from another parish came to live in Wye, the parish would take steps to send them home again before they became the responsibility of Wye. The overseers would apply to the Justices for an order authorising them to send the strangers back to their own parish. They would first have to present evidence to establish where the family's legal settlement was, and the parish to which they proposed to send them might challenge this evidence, and so barristers and solicitors would be involved.

Thus, for example, in 1732 the overseers recorded that -

Pd for carrying Lent, Stockwell and goodwife Hollands to the sitting at Ashford	5/6d
gave goodman Lent	5/0d
Pd Counsellor Knowler & Counsellor Toke for Tryall about goodman Lent	£2/2/0d
ffor 3 journeys to Canterbury for Council	12/0d

---

[1] The topic of settlement occupies 110 pages in Burn's *Justice of the Peace and Parish Officer* (10th edition, 1776).

pd for a warrant   1/0d
pd for a Sessions Order   5/0d

In a similar case in 1737 two barristers, John Knowler, the Recorder of Canterbury, and Charles Robinson, who later became the Recorder and Member of Parliament, were retained at a cost of nine pounds to appear on behalf of the Parish.[1]

The trouble and expense involved in such cases arising out of the law of settlement may be illustrated by the case of Widow Austen (or Austing) in 1734. It appears that she and her children were living in Wye, but their legal settlement was in Oxford. So the overseers of Wye had to get her sent back to Oxford.

Pd for Horse and man to carry Jane Austing to the sitting at Ashford[2]   2/0d
Pd for a horse and man at Ashford for coming to Wye to fetch her certificate   2/0d
Pd for an order to remove her and her children to Oxford   4/0d
Pd Jane Austing 3 weeks pay, Due Oct 19th   9/0d
Jane Austing more weeks pay   9/0d
Gave her and her children to Canterbury   5/0d
Pd Robert Dan for going to Oxford   £5/13/11d

Sometimes however a mistake was made. In 1788 the overseer records that he spent £2/8/3d on getting a Court Order for removal of Hannah Monday to St Lawrence near Ramsgate, and then taking her there. But the next entry is -

Journey to St Lawrence about Hannah Monday's being removed there by Mistake instead of being removed to Ramsgate the Place of her Settlement. (Ramsgate *Town* or *Parish* maintaining their own poor).[3]   19/5d

This system of the overseers obtaining an order of the court for the removal of people to the parish of their settlement proved unsatisfactory; it was expensive, and it restricted the mobility of labour, preventing labourers from finding employment where work was available and where labour was needed. So, in 1795 an act[4] was passed, limiting the power of the courts to make orders of removal to cases where the people in question were actually in need of parochial relief.

More often the overseers would encourage strangers to go away voluntarily, with a shilling or two to help them on their way. If they were sick (as

---

[1] In the overseer's accounts instead of "retained" the parish clerk wrote several times "detained". Charles Robinson was the brother of Matthew Robinson Morris (later Lord Rokeby) who had a long white beard which at election time he dyed blue, to indicate his political allegiance, (see *The History of Parliament*, House of Commons, 1754-1790, pp. 363,367)

[2] i.e. the Petty Sessions.

[3] The mistake is excusable. According to Hasted's *History of Kent* "The Ville of Ramsgate, though in the parish of St Lawrence, yet maintains its own poor separately . . . It is within the Liberty of the Cinque Ports, being an ancient member of the town and port of Sandwich."

[4] 35 Geo. III, c.101

many of them were), they would be looked after until they were fit to travel, but the overseers were always anxious to get rid of them, lest they should acquire a settlement in the parish, and so become potentially a financial liability.

If however the strangers were intending to stay for a short time, perhaps to help in the harvest, they would bring with them a certificate from their own parish, guaranteeing that if they became chargeable to the poor law, that parish would accept responsibility for them. These certificates, duly signed and sealed by the churchwardens and overseers, attested by two credible witnesses and signed by two Justices, were carefully recorded in the "Certificate Book" of both the parishes concerned. Arrangements could sometimes be made for a poor person to live permanently in Wye (perhaps a widow returning to the parish where she was born) while being supported financially by the overseers of another parish. Thus for many years the overseers of Withyham in Sussex regularly reimbursed the parish of Wye for the maintenance of Widow Inkpen, whose legal settlement was in Withyham, but who lived in Wye. Similar arrangements were made for some people with settlements in Wye to live in other parishes but yet to be supported by the overseers of Wye.

A married woman took her settlement from her husband; a child automatically took its settlement from its father, but a bastard child, having legally no father, took its settlement from the parish in which it was born. The overseers of that parish would be anxious to avoid the expense of maintaining such a child, and so would try to get the parents married before the child was born, thus giving it the settlement of the father. Hence the marriage of many reluctant fathers (or alleged fathers), often at the expense of the parish.

A case of this sort arose in Wye in 1704, and the overseer, Richard Jarman, records

For a licence and fetching John Marsh	£1/2/0d
Gave a man to take him	17/6d
Spent when he was brought to the Saracen's Head	10/0d
For my Horse hire and Expense	12/0d
For my Horsehire and expenses Gave a man to go	12/6d
Gave a man to goe from Buckland to New Romney for him	1/0d
Gave the Person for marrying him	2/6d

Or again, later in the century -

Journey to Binchell to take up Thos Hobday & Expenses of his examination to his Settlement, marrying him to Mary Kennett & Carrying Home to the Parish of Elham
£5/13/3½d
Paid Mr Oliver which he lent Thomas Hobday at the time he was married   £6/0/0d

Bastardy problems arose regularly, and it was not always possible to get the alleged parents married in time, before the child was born. If this proved impossible the overseers would try, not always successfully, to get from the father either a single sum of £10 or £15, or a regular monthly payment.

In 1786 there were several such entries -

Expenses at the Flying Horse when John Kennett[1] was in custody for Bastard Child
11/5d

Thomas Quested,[2] Constable, for his trouble	6/0d
Mary Moon 3 weeks for her Bastard Child	6/0d
Gave her in her sickness at Several Times	£1/9/6d
Journey to Canterbury with Thomas Quested, Constable, to apprehend Mackenzie for a Bastard Child Sworn to him by Mary Vidgen. Horsehire and Expenses and the Constable's Charges attending the same	18/4d
Journey to the Sessions - Horsehire and Expenses to appear against Mackenzie when he was continued on his Recognizances till the next Quarter Sessions	6/2d
Journey Horsehire and Expenses to Quarter Sessions at Canterbury with Mary Vidgen	11/5d
Paid the Clerk of the Peace for the Sessions Order made on James Mackenzie for the Lying in of the said Mary Vidgen and the maintenance of the child	8/4d

Such entries were commonplace in the next few years. In one case, after the putative father had been found at Chilham, there was a further expense for "Two men sitting up with him all night at the Flying Horse at Wye (By Mr Sawbridge's order)".

It was not always easy to find defaulting fathers, and in March 1765 the vestry resolved to put an advertisement in the Canterbury papers -

Whereas William Scrims, alias Buck, Labourer did some time since Run away from his Family, he is about 5 feet 6 inches high, of a fair Complexion and about 48 years of Age. If he will return again to his Family immediately or within fourteen days from the Date above he will be forgiven, otherwise whoever will apprehend him and bring him to the Parish Officers of Wye shall receive One Guinea Reward.

William Scrims was apparently located, and perhaps forgiven. On the 20th of April 1766 the vestry resolved unanimously that -

[1] In 1779 the Wye Vestry had agreed to provide for John Kennett the son of William Kennett at Brook (a parishioner of Wye) the necessary clothes to enable him to go into service with Mr Tunbridge of Hastingleigh. Clothes were also provided for the other children of William Kennett. It is not clear how, or whether, they were related to William Kennett of Wye Court.

[2] Thomas Quested senior was a maltster, Thomas Quested junior a clocksmith.

George Elliott Esqre at Wombwell Hall near Gravesend should pay or Cause to be paid the sum of two shillings per Week to the Overseers of the Poor of the Parish of Wye in the County of Kent towards the maintaining of William Scrim's (his Servant) Wife and Family as long as the said William Scrims should live with the aforesaid George Elliott Esqre the said payment to commence from the 17th day of April 1766.

The overseers' accounts show that this was duly paid. Twenty years later another problem of a defaulting husband arose -

Journey to Brookland Isle of Oxney, Self and Horse to find Beale a Sawyer who run away and left his Family Chargeable to this Parish	13/0d
For a Horse for Quested, Constable, going to the afore mentioned Place	5/0d
George Beale's Wife and 4 children in Want at several Times.	13/0d
Journey to the Committee at Ashford with Mrs Beale to be examined in Respect to her Settlement Examination. Order of Removal and Copy & Expenses	6/0d
Henry Part for Lodging, Fire, and Candle for Mrs Beale and Family	5/0d
Journey to Chatham with Mrs Beale & Family Horsehire and Expenses	£1/4/6d
Rayner for carrying them to Chatham in his Cart	£1/1/0d

In 1733 there came to Wye two women, Moll Day and "the Wench that liv'd at Vincer's." They were commonly referred to as "the hors" or "the Whors" but none the less, as they were in need, the overseers looked after them.

Among the entries in the Poor Book, under the heading "Disbursements Extraordinary", there are such entries as -

ffor carrying Moll[1] Day to Counsellor Toke to be examined	3/6d
ffor going to Kennington to get Moll Day's child registd	1/0d
Moll Day and the Wench that liv'd at Vincer's	6/0d
Pd goodw. Rainer 4 weeks Lodging for Moll Day	4/0d
Pd goodw. Austen for Wench came from Vincers	7/0d
Pd Moll Day 4 weeks with her Bastard	6/0d
Pd the other Whore 4 weeks with her Bastard	6/0d
Pd both the whor's 2 weeks pay more	6/0d
Pd goodw. Rainer more for Lodging & nursing Moll Day	£1/1/0d
Pd goodw. Austen for nursing the Whors Moll Day and She that liv'd at Vincer's	£1/8/0d
Gave the Creature at Bodkins	2/0d
Pd Vincer's Moll for doing for Goody Austen 3 weeks	1/6d

In 1744 further entries appear among the "Disbursements Extraordinary" -

gave Stephen Beale for enlarging Richard Dryland's Coat	2/0d
gave Robert Hunt's wife and family when he went of for fear	1/0d

[1] Moll was a word for a prostitute in the 18th century.

gave her more when he was of for fear of being prest	2/0d
Pd Mr John Weller constable wn Robert Hunt was seized	£1/1/0d
gave Robt Hunt's Family several times in want	15/0d

Presumably Robert Hunt was afraid of being taken by the press gang for the Navy.

In 1737 a question arose about the Drewry family, with a settlement in Wye, but living in Canterbury. The Wye overseers were responsible for them and were instructed by the vestry to pay them ten shillings. This involved a journey to Canterbury costing 6d, but the Canterbury overseers sent the family back to Wye, at a cost of £1/16/1d. As they were destitute the Wye overseers gave them 2/3d, and also a leg of mutton and 3d worth of small beer, two pairs of sheets, a bed, a spade, 100 faggots and occasional grants of money. The overseers also from then on paid their rent, of two pounds a year, to Mr Kennett of Wye Court.

In 1753 the overseers paid Thomas Drewry two pounds "for his Mother having the small pox". Her illness proved fatal, and her son was then paid nineteen shillings for burying her.

Many of the entries refer to the burial of parishioners, often including the cost of beer for the men who dug the grave and carried the coffin. There were also payments for wool in which the dead had to be buried. By the Act 30 Charles II c. 3 (1679) no one might be buried except in sheep's wool - a regulation aimed at encouraging the wool trade.[1]

Sometimes the cost of the funeral was set out in full, as, for example, in 1722 -

Pd for breaking ground for Sarah Moons Child, etc	2/8d
Pd for the Knell and tolling the Bell	2/6d
Pd for the Minister for Reading the Buriall	2/6d
Pd the Clerk for Laying the boy forth	2/0d
Pd for the Affidavit (certifying that the body was buried in wool) and for Beer	4/6d
Pd for my Horses standing	2d

Most of the expenditure by the overseers was for the immediate necessities of the poor of the village, or on temporary relief for strangers passing through. They did, however, from time to time disburse larger sums to provide a craftsman with his tools, or more often, to give a poor man or woman a cow or a horse. It appears that in some cases the cow was hired by a parishioner at the rate of twelve shillings a year. There are also entries for

---

[1] The Sawbridges were usually buried in linen, being willing to pay the penalty for this privilege.

the expenses of driving the cow to Waltham (8d) and a year later for fetch-
ing it back to Wye (1/0d), after which the overseer apparently kept it for a
time, charging two shillings a week to the Poor Sess. In 1772 the overseers
paid £5/13/0d "towards buying a bullock for the poor".

In 1770 the overseers gave Edward Rayner the sum of £2/12/6d to buy a
horse. A few months later the accounts record that they paid four shillings
and six pence to Dr Taylor, the parish physician, "for curing Edward
Rayner's Horse".

One person who caused the overseers considerable trouble was John
Jarman, probably a descendant of William Jarman who in 1479 bequeathed
his field, which still bears his name, for the maintenance of the church. In
1730 the overseer, Thomas Parker, recorded -

> Pd Mr Hawling four pounds four shillings and six pence by Jacob Sawbridge Esquire
> for Clothing of John Jarman in the Mad House.

It appears that Jarman did not stay in the mad house, as in the following
year there are further references to him -

> Pd Samson ffarbrace for keeping Jarman at 7/0d per week   £2/16/0d
> Paid Samson Farbrace for keeping John Jarman Eight weeks more at 7/0d per
> week   £2/16/0d
> My expenses going to London to fetch Jarman home   £5/9/0d
> Pd George Gillett when he brought Jarman's money from London   1/0d

The next reference to John Jarman is in 1732, when the Vestry agreed
to indemnify Robert Dan for "taking John Jarman our Lunatick man into
the Hospital of Incurables at Bethlehem". There, at Bethlehem Hospital
(alias Bedlam) he remained for some years, the overseers paying for his
maintenance, which amounted in 1735 to £14/7/0d and in 1736 to
£8/13/0d. In that year Thomas Paine, the overseer, recorded in his
accounts -

> Item Recd back from the Hospital for Mad John Jarman being Dead by the
> hand of George Gillett the sum   £3/19/0d
> Pd George Gillett when he brought Jarman's money from London   1/0d

An example of how the overseers presented their accounts may be taken
from the account of James Watt in 1737.

Brought over	111	05	08¾
P: Mr. Doughton making an order to remove Margaret Cook to Woodchurch	000	03	00
Expences man & horses &c to Woodchurch wth her	000	11	00
gave the Parks in illness	000	02	00
p: for a Lre from Canterbury	000	00	0f
p: making 2 pare of Sheets for Drewry	000	01	04
gave Sprott and wife more in illness	000	01	00
p: for 2 an hundred Fagg: for Drewry	000	07	00
gave Matt: Court 12 & Drewry more 12	000	02	00
P: Robt: Warham carrying wood to Drewrys	000	02	00
P: for Law: Whithead 12 emd Drewry more 12	000	02	06
P: more for goodw: Chapmans Lodging	000	04	00
gave goodm: Drewry more	000	01	00
p: for woosted for the girle at Finches	000	00	06
p: more for Law: Whithead Lodging	000	01	00
p: goodw: for looking to Drewrys family	001	00	00
gave Sprott & wife &c 2.6 & Drewry & family man 1:6	000	05	00
p: the Minister for burying John Skilton	000	01	00
p: for laying him forth	000	01	00
gave goodm: Drewry more in want	000	01	00
p: more for Law: Whithead Lodging	000	01	00
p: for washing baking & removing John Skilton	000	02	00
p: more for Lodging of Law: Whithead	000	01	00
p: goodw: for doing for goodw: Ja: Austen	000	00	06
Gave Patmore at coming home	000	00	06
Gave Matt: Court more in want	000	01	00
p: more for goodm: Whitheads Lodging	000	01	00
p: Sampson Garbrace for Patmore	000	05	00
gave goodm: Skilton on the bank	000	01	00
P: Sampson Garbrace for 5: had for Skilton	000	04	04
P: Wm: Philpott for a Bed for Drewry	000	03	00
P: for goodw: Chapmans Lodging	000	04	00
	116	05	11¾

During much of the eighteenth century the Army was engaged in India, America and Europe. During the Seven Years War, for example, there are several references to soldiers and their families passing through Wye, and being helped on their way by small gifts from the parish overseers.

At the end of the century, during the war with France, the parish authorities were more involved, being responsible for preparing the lists of men liable to be conscripted into the Militia. (Peers, clergymen, members of the universities, apprentices, and poor men with three or more children born in wedlock were exempt). This involved some expenditure on making out the lists, and travelling to Ashford to present them. The arrangements for recruiting for the Navy were different. The "Press Gang" played a major part in this, but there are also entries in the Poor Book showing that in 1794 a payment was made of £56/16/0d "for raising men for Navy", but apparently the arrangements went wrong, as two years later there is another entry - "forfeit for not raising 3 men for Navy, £61/10/6½".

The parish was also responsible for the support of the families of the militia men who were called to the colours. But it was open to those who were called to find instead a substitute. This involved some expenditure for the parish -

> Paid John Marsh for Swearing himself a Substitute in the Militia for Thomas
> Else   £1/16/0d

In 1780 and subsequent years the enrolment of substitutes for the Militia became more common, with increased cost to the parish -

> Pd Militia Substitutes W.Macay   £4/4/0d
> Pd Militia Substitutes George Pack   £5/0/0d
> Paid towards a Substitute in the Militia for Mr Hudson   £5/0/0d
> Received of the Parish Officers of Wittersham for the maintenance of
> the Wife and Children of John Gurney, Mason, a substitute in the
> East Kent Regiment of Militia, at 4/6d per week   £8/2/0d

In the next year there was an entry -

> Paid for Militia Substitutes for Richd Vincer, Jas. Holton, Stephn Pack
> and John Miller, £5/0/0d each   £20/0/0d

It might be assumed that the soldiers were only in Wye as they travelled from place to place, but there are some entries which suggest that some of them stayed here for some time. There are a number of entries for payments to soldiers for such services as "making Cloathes for Master Dunn in the Workhouse", and "for a Smock Frock for Peter Hubbard."

There is no apparent explanation why soldiers were employed in this way.

Peter Hubbard was a poor boy of the parish. On 10 June 1780 the vestry had ordered that -

> Peter Hubbard shall have a Coat and Waistcoat and shall live with Mr Brett for a Year from the 24th Instant, the Parish agreeing to find him in Cloaths of all sorts during the said Term - the said Mr Brett allowing him Pocket Money.[1]

In addition to the soldiers, passing through Wye on their way to join their regiments, a number of sailors passed through Wye, probably on their way to join their ships at Dover. They travelled with a pass - a document issued by the Justices requiring overseers of the poor in parishes through which they passed to help them on their way.[2]

One entry which occurs regularly in the overseers' accounts relates to the payment of "Goal Money". This had nothing to do with football, but was the contribution of the parish to the expenses of the county authority - the Quarter Sessions. They had many functions in addition to their judicial duties, including the conveyance of soldiers' baggage, inspection of weights and measures, and, most expensive of all, the county gaols at Maidstone and Canterbury. It was usual throughout the county to refer to this contribution as the "Goal Money", or sometimes as the "Gole Money".

Another function covered by Goal Money was the maintenance of the county bridges. But not all bridges were included in this. Some, such as Shalmsford Bridge, down river from Wye, were the responsibility of the hundred; some, as at Canterbury, were maintained by the City or Borough Corporation, and some, like the Sparrow Bridge below Olantigh and the Bridge at Godmersham, were the responsibility of the parish. This fact was firmly proclaimed by the inscription on Godmersham Bridge -

> This Bridge was built By the Parish and Not By the County 1698 Thomas Carter and Richard Austen Surweighers

In contrast with this, the bridge at Wye bore the inscription

> This Bridge was built at the only charge of the County of Kent in ye yeare 1638 and repaired att the only Charge of ye said County in ye yeare 1683 John Marshe, Gent, George Simmons, gent, Henry Coulter and John Kennet being Surveyors and Expeditors John Bigge and John Taylor John Bigge Junior Alexander Butcher Caleb Bigge James Taster, workmen.

---

[1] In 1788 there was an entry "Elliott at Waters Corner for taking care of Peter Hubbard when he fell from the Waggon - 1/0".

[2] Provision was made for soldiers and sailors to travel freely through the country provided they had a pass from a Magistrate or from their officers, by the Vagrancy Act, 17 George II, c.5..

In 1764 the Wye Bridge was presented at the Quarter Sessions as being in need of repair. Two magistrates were appointed to inspect the bridge and report. They were John Sawbridge of Olantigh, and Nicholas Brett of Spring Grove, both inhabitants of Wye. They reported that work was needed; £103/0/2d was then spent out of the county stock.

One enigmatic entry which recurs a number of times in the 1780s is -

Paid Mary Cobb more for Schooling for Hatton Finch   2/2d

and in 1781 and 1782 -

For a Book for Hatton Finch   6d

It is not clear why the parish should have paid for the education of this child, when there were two endowed schools in the village, where education was free. Moreover, according to Hasted's *History of Kent*[1], Daniel Finch, Earl of Winchilsea and Lord of the Manor of Wye had a daughter, christened Hatton. It is not apparent whether this is the same person as the one who was being educated at the expense of the poor rate, but dates suggest that it is not.[2] On 6 May 1781 the vestry decided to give Hatton Finch a coat, waistcoat and breeches, so it appears that Hatton was a boy. In 1827 and subsequent years Hatton Finch appears in the Surveyors' accounts, for carting stones for the repair of the roads.

In 1792 there is an entry in the Overseers' Accounts -

For Advertising the Resolutions of the Inhabitants agreed upon at a
Meeting concerning Tom Pain   5/2d

This was immediately after the publication of Thomas Paine's "Rights of Man", which was regarded with horror up and down the country, though presumably not at Olantigh, the home of the radical Member of Parliament, John Sawbridge, and of his sister, Catherine Macaulay, "the Republican Virago", who died the year before.

The advertisement duly appeared in the Kentish Gazette on the 4th of January, 1793, in these words -

WYE

Thomas Brett in the chair

At a numerous meeting of the inhabitants of the parish the following declaration was unanimously agreed to:

---

[1] Vol. VII, Page 408.

[2] His other daughters were Heneage, Essex and Augusta,

Partakers in that love for our King and Constitution which we see with peculiar pleasure animate the kingdom in general, and sensible to the blessings we enjoy are by no human means more likely to be continued to us than by cordial unanimity and peaceful association - we, the inhabitants of Wye, do hereby readily join the public voice, and heartily unto so declaring our inviolable attachment to the Constitution established in King, Lords and Commons; and further we declare that we will endeavour, as far as in our power, to preserve and promote the public peace and discourage every tendency to slot and sedition (sic).

At the time the thanks of the Meeting were unanimously given to the Chairman for the very proper and social conduct in the business of the evening, and for his generous attention to the wants of the poor.

Dated Monday Dec. 31st 1792.

Similar, and often more grammatical, resolutions were passed in a number of other parishes, it being widely feared that the policies advocated by Tom Paine would lead in England to a revolution and the execution of the King. In Wye, after the close of the meeting, beer was distributed, and a subscription was collected for the poor.

The Vestry

For the years between 1747 and 1762 there is no record of how often the vestry met nor what it did, but from 1762 there are regular minutes of the meetings. This coincides with the appointment of the Rev. Philip Parsons as perpetual curate of Wye and Master of the Grammar School. He was also Rector of Snave and of Eastwell, and domestic chaplain to Lord Sondes. He remained in Wye for fifty years, living in the college and devoting much of his time to writing on such subjects as stained glass, racing at Newmarket, astronomy, and Sunday Schools. In 1770 he contemplated resigning the mastership of the school in favour of the Rev. Joseph Price, who was attracted by the idea of living in the college, having the school as a sinecure, and perhaps taking over the Flying Horse, but like Price's other schemes it came to nothing.

Despite his varied offices Philip Parsons was a conscientious attender at the vestry meetings in Wye. Part of the business was directly related to the Church, dealing with the allotment of pews, the appointment of the sexton and other such matters, but most of the entries in the minutes refer to the relief of the poor. There were very few duties assigned by statute to the vestry, though, by the Act 3 William III c.12 "the Constables, Churchwardens, Surveyors of Highways and Inhabitants in every parish" were to assemble once a year and prepare a list of people qualified to be appointed surveyors of highways. From this list the Justices were to choose the surveyor for the coming year.

In the words of Beatrice and Sidney Webb "to the parish officers the Vestry meeting stood in a doubtful relation. In the appointment of the Constable and the Overseers of the Poor the inhabitants had legally no share; their statutory participation was of the shadowest; while over the expenditure of all these officers or of the rate which they levied, they had absolutely no control".

None the less the vestry of Wye came to exercise considerable authority in practice. They gave instructions to the overseers on many occasions; they authorised the building of new galleries and pews in the church; they decided to sell the poor house, and to establish a workhouse and a pest house; they appointed the masters of both these institutions; they entered into contracts with tradesmen to take parish boys as apprentices, and into contracts with doctors to treat the poor of the parish; they decreed what clothes should be provided for the children of the poor, and they gave instructions about the repair of the roads. In short, they became the general rulers of the village.

Nowhere was it laid down who should be members of the vestry, but it was clearly understood that only the more substantial parishioners were entitled to attend. Unlike most of the parishes of Kent there was no squire of Wye, though the owners of Olantigh had many of the characteristics of a squire; they owned much of the property of the village, and a large part of the agricultural land, but they were not lords of the manor, and on account of their political views they had not the full status of squirehood; they were too eccentric.

In the early part of the century Jacob Sawbridge of Olantigh often attended the vestry meetings. He was a banker, and from 1715 to 1721 he was a Member of Parliament. He had bought the estate from the trustees of Richard Thornhill (grandson of Lady Joanna, the founder of the school at Wye). He was also a director of the South Sea Company, and when the "South Sea Bubble" burst in 1721 he was expelled from Parliament, and committed to the custody of the Serjeant at Arms. Most of his property was forfeited, but he managed to retain the Olantigh estate until he died in 1748, leaving it to his son John Sawbridge. It then passed in 1762 to the second John Sawbridge, who occasionally attended the vestry meetings, and served as surveyor of highways for Wye from 1764 to 1766. After that time he was probably too busy in London to spend much time in Wye; he was a partner with his father-in-law as a hop merchant and distiller, was an alderman of the City of London, Sheriff in 1768 and Lord Mayor in 1775. He was also a Member of Parliament from 1768 until his death in 1795[1].

Politically he was a determined radical, actively supporting John Wilkes in his demand for shorter Parliaments, electoral reform and conciliation in America. His sister was Catherine Macaulay[2], whose egalitarian principles aroused the wit of Dr Johnson, and whose historical books had considerable influence on the French writers who stimulated the French Revolution.

[1] For the Sawbridges see *The History of Parliament*, the House of Commons, 1715-1754 and 1754-1790.
[2] For Catherine Macaulay see Bridget Hill, *The Republican Virago*.

Others who commonly attended the vestry meetings were Valentine Austen, a maltster, and his son, also Valentine[1] and Nicholas Brett, son of Thomas Brett the non-juring bishop who inherited the Spring Grove estate, and his son, also Nicholas. The family most often represented at vestry meetings was the Kennetts of Wye Court, and of Bramble and Harville Farms. Other regular members were the Philpotts, Dans and Questeds. Some times only three of four people attended the meetings.

This small group was not only the mainstay of the vestry; they also served in turn as the parish officers, as churchwardens, overseers, surveyors of the highways, and as constables. The labourers and poorer villagers did not attend the vestry, nor, as a rule did women, though on two occasions towards the end of the century, a woman was there - one of them illiterate, and signing the minutes "Margaret Gratnall X her mark".

One man who owned much of the land in Wye in the early part of the century was John Hopkins, commonly called "Vulture Hopkins" on account of his rapacity. He made a great fortune by speculation, especially in the South Sea Bubble, and sat in Parliament for St Ives from 1710 to 1715 and for Ilchester from 1715 to 1722. In 1732 he died, worth £300,000, having made a will of extreme complexity. Among his properties were Wye Court, Harville, Coldharbour, Wye Downs and Naccolt. As he did not live in Wye he did not play a part in the local government of the parish.

On the death of John Hopkins his estate passed to a distant relative, Benjamin Bond, an attorney's clerk in London. He then adopted the name of Bond Hopkins, and became the Member of Parliament for Ilchester and then for Malmesbury. He sold the estates in Wye to John Sawbridge, who thereby came to own, according to Hasted, almost half the parish.[2]

The earliest surviving minute book begins in 1724, and the first entry in it asserts the claim of the vestry to regulate the business of the village -

> It was agreed at the Vestry that no one Officer should have the Privilege of giving away to the Parishioners any Sum or Sums of money as is specified in the Last Account and some Before passed without consent of two proper Officers on such cases provided for by consent of a Public Vestry without incurring the penalty of paying the same out of his own proper Stock. Further without an Extraordinary Occasion no Doctor to be employed and that the Parish be acquainted with Clothing of the Poor.

---

[1] The peculiar procedure of his funeral is described in Morris's *History of Wye* pp. 84-86.
[2] For Benjamin Bond Hopkins see the *Gentleman's Magazine*, 1794 pp. 183, 184, 200, 275, and *The History of Parliament*, 1754-90, p100.

Soon afterwards the vestry again exercised its authority -

Memorandum

It was agreed that no Overseer should have the Privilege of Spending above four Shillings for Beer at any ffuneral of the Poor without incurring the Penalty of paying the same out of his own stock, etc.

The resolution about employing a doctor was intended, it appears, to prevent the overseers calling the doctor for merely routine consultation. The vestry did however enter into contracts with local practitioners for medical attention to the poor as occasion arose.

In 1729, for example, the vestry passed a resolution relating to Peter Morell, a local doctor -

By order of the Vestry this Day held in the Parish of Wye it was agreed that Nath. Miles Overseer should agree with Mr. Peter Morell that wt Poor are or shall belong to the said Parish of Wye or be allowed weekly Collection or have the Rents of their Houses paid by the Parish or shall live in any alm's Houses belonging to the said Parish, and shall have any Sort of Sickness, Disease or Lameness shall have all sorts of Physick and Chirurgical Operation Administered to them at the Charge of the Said Mr Morell and performed til Lady Day next for the sum of two Guineas which the Vestry hereby Promise to pay to him for the same the said Mr Morell not to be obliged to attend any Person out of the bounds of said Parish.

Memorandum

The said Mr Morell Sign'd this Order not to attend Broken Bones to be included into the same Sum aforesaid, etc.

In subsequent agreements with doctors the method of payment was changed to a *per capita* system - one shilling a year for each poor person living in the town of Wye, two shillings for those living outside the town, but in the parish. For twenty four years the doctor so employed was William Scudamore[1], who served also as the family doctor for the Knights of Godmersham, where he came to know Edward Knight's sister, Jane Austen. He was described on his tombstone in Wye churchyard as "sober, grave, temperate, sound in faith, in charity, in patience".

As the century advanced the vestry met more regularly - often at fortnightly or even weekly intervals. It also became more involved in the day to day business of the Poor Law; it regularly gave orders to the overseers,

1 See M. Lane, Jane Austen's Family p.167. When Godmersham House was repainted Jane wrote to Henry Austen that "Mr Scudamore is very decided as to Godmersham not being fit to be inhabited at present - he talks even of two months to sweeten it . . . My brother will probably go down and sniff at it himself and receive his rents". See also Dictionary of National Biography under Sir Charles Scudamore (his son).

instructing them to provide shoes for children, clothes or wood for widows. On the 19th of December, 1779, for example, it resolved -

> Agreed in Vestry to give Mary Quested a gown, two shifts, a pair of shoes, pair of Stockings and Handkerchief; at the same time agree to Cloathe the two natural Children of Thos Beaver's Wife, Also to Cloathe Thos Smeed the Younger.

A week later they met again, with the Revd Philip Parsons again in the chair, and decided to give the daughter of Widow Jakes a pair of stays, gown, flannel petticoat and two shifts.

The compassionate attitude of the parish authorities is shown also in the arrangements for training the youths of the village. The vestry arranged and paid for a number of boys to be apprenticed to tradesmen in Kent or in London. This had the incidental advantage that they thereby acquired a new settlement in the parish where they served their apprenticeship and so ceased to be the responsibility of the parish of Wye. On the 22nd September, 1769 the vestry considered the case of William Rew -

> At Vestry this day holden by the Churchwarden and Overseer together with the principle Inhabitants we, whose names are hereunto Subscribed do Agree that the Overseers of the said Parish shall find a Place for the Widow Rew's son to be put out as an Apprentice to a periwig maker or some Sitting Business he not being able to do hard Labour.
>
> Philip Parsons Curate   Nic Brett
> Wm Laming   Wm Kennett

There then follows a note -

> He was put out Apprentice by this Parish to Robt Sandford of Folkestone Perukemaker for 7 years commencing from 15 January 1770.

Indentures of apprenticeship were then completed, and £10/0/0d paid to Mr Sandford, but soon afterward another entry was made in the Vestry Book recording that -

> His Mother not being able to find him in Cloathes during his Apprenticeship (although she had covenanted so to do in the said Indentures). It is hereby agreed that the Churchwardens and Overseers of the said Parish of Wye and their successors for the time being shall and will find and Provide for the said William Rew competent and sufficient Wearing Apparel of all sorts fit for such an Apprentice to have and wear during the said Term of Seven Years.

But eighteen months later there is another minute in the book -

> It is further agreed by the Vestry that the Overseers for the Time Being shall make Immediate Application to His Majesty's Justices of the Peace for this County against the Widow Rew and Laurence Tucker both of this Parish for harbouring Idle and

Disorderly Persons Contrary to Law and also Bringing an Expense on the Parish in Relieving such Idle disorderly Persons.

None the less after this the Widow Rew appears on the list of recipients of parish relief.

The Workhouse

The squire of the neighbouring parish of Brabourne, Sir Edward Knatchbull, who often allowed (i.e. authorised) the accounts of the Wye overseers, sat in Parliament for the County of Kent for a number of years[1]. In 1723 he introduced a bill to enable church wardens and overseers of a parish to provide a workhouse. This bill was passed with some amendments and was known as Knatchbull's Act, or more formally as 9 George I, c.7. A number of Kentish parishes adopted the scheme in the course of the next twenty or thirty years. It is however not clear at what date Wye first established a workhouse under this Act. The Parliamentary Returns of 1776 show the establishment of a workhouse here in 1762, but there is evidence of there being one some years earlier. Unfortunately the vestry minutes are incomplete for the first half of the century.

In 1742 the accounts of the overseers, Thomas Hudson and William Kennett, include a number of references to a workhouse in the village -

> Pd Mr William Dann for a Copper Cooking Back and other goods and a tub of Pork which he sold for the use of the Poor in the Workhouse from Mr May's Sale of Crundale as by bill appears £9/9/6d
> Pd Thomas Peck for a hemp comb for the Workhouse 5/0d
> Pd Ed Beeching for a Barrell of Beer for the Workhouse 3/1d
> Pd Thomas Beeching for setting on hoops at the Workhouse 5/0d
> Pd Mr Elvie for 29 lbs of Cheese at 2d for the Workhouse 6/6d
> Pd Mr Richd Kennett for Brewing Tub for the Workhouse £1/0/0d
> Spent at the Time the Parish met about hiring the Workhouse 5/0d
> Spent on Workmen working about the Workhouse 1/0d
> Pd Mr Vincer for Meet for the Poor House 4/6d
> Pd Wm Hunt for meat for the same 11/3d

It thus seems that a workhouse had been established by 1743. In that year for the first time there appears in the overseer's accounts a separate statement of the cost of running the workhouse. Each month two of the "Principal Inhabitants" were appointed as trustees of the workhouse responsible for the management and expenditure. For example, the first such entries in the Poor Book are -

---

[1] For Sir Edward Knatchbull see Sir Hughe Knatchbull-Hugesson, *Kentish Family* pp. 121 - 136.

May 1743 pd Mr Wm Kennett and Mr Thomas Back	£11/3/6d
June the 7th pd Mr John Atwood and Mr Richard Kennett	£8/2/5d
July the 5th pd Mr Nat. Miles and Mr John Paine	£17/12/7d

The "Town Map" of 1746 shows the workhouse on the North side of Bridge Street, opposite the almshouses. It also shows the "Poor House" in Upper Bridge Street, at the junction with "Oxen Pond Lane".[1] This house, formally called Puntowes, had been given to the parish by Robert Searles, a clergyman, in 1570.[2] It was sometimes known as "Searles Hospital", and was held by the parish as a charitable trust. There was also a separate trust, established by Thomas Boys in 1625, to pay 13/4d a year, charged on land at Naccolt, for the benefit of the inhabitants of Puntowes. There was no attempt to set the inhabitants of Puntowes to work; it was rather a home for the aged and the poor.

When the workhouse in Lower Bridge Street was established in 1743 the building was rented from Thomas Braybrook,[3] a carpenter, for five guineas a year. Twenty years later the vestry decided to buy the freehold of the house, and to raise the necessary money by selling the "Poor House" (alias Puntowes). Whether the vestry was acting legally in thus disposing of property bequeathed for a charitable purpose was a question which was not apparently considered, but which caused some difficulty in the next century.[4]

In the new workhouse, unlike the old "Poor House", the inhabitants were expected to do some work. This was not a new idea in Wye; in 1622 Henry Haule of Maidstone had given by his will the sum of £20 to be employed upon some hemp, flax, wool or other such matters, to employ the poor children and aged persons of the parish in work, so that out of the increase of it they should have some recompense for their labour. This however did not involve any degree of discipline or residence in a workhouse, such as were imposed in the new institution in Lower Bridge Street.

The vestry minutes record that in 1762 Joseph Wright and his wife were appointed to manage the workhouse and to put the inhabitants to work on spinning worsted. There were about twenty paupers living in the house, while most of the poor continued to be relieved in their own homes.

[1] In *The Old Book of Wye* Hubbard identifies the Poor House with the buildings which now house the Public Library and the Wife of Bath restaurant.

[2] For details of Robert Searles see Hubbard, *The Old Book of Wye*, pp.154-7 and D. Ingram Hill, *The Six Preachers of Canterbury Cathedral*, p.12.

[3] Thomas Braybrook was overseer in 1741 and 1742.

[4] There is an unexplained entry in the Overseer's Accounts in 1755 - "Spent at Robert Questeds wn ye workhouse was bought - 11/-"

In 1768 Mr and Mrs Wright left the workhouse, and were succeeded by Thomas Pack and John Clements, who were specifically instructed to see that the inhabitants were properly employed. Within a year Pack and Clements had both left, and the workhouse was "Destitute of a Master". A new Master and Mistress, Richard and Elizabeth Scott, were appointed to fill the vacancy. In May 1787, the vestry resolved that -

> The Overseers of the Poor shall provide Spinning Wheels and other implements and Necessaries at the expense of the Parish for the Purpose of Employing the Poor Children in the Workhouse and other Poor Children belonging to the Parish in Spinning and also Employing them in Knitting and other work, which the Parish shall think fit and the Expense attending the same shall be paid by the Overseers of the Poor of the said Parish for the time being and to be allowed for in their Accounts and what the Children shall earn shall be brought to the Credit Account of the said Overseers.

Arrangements were then made to borrow £100 for the purchase of wool "for the purpose of employing the Poor in the Workhouse and other Poor Inhabitants belonging to the said Parish in Spinning thereof." It was also agreed that the children so employed should be allowed one penny in the shilling of the income from their spinning and knitting.

This attempt to put the poor to work and at the same time bring in more revenue to balance the books appears to have been a failure.

Seven months later, on the 18th November, 1787 the Vestry returned to the subject -

> It appears unto us whose names are hereunto Subscribed upon Trial thereof made that continuing to carry on the Spinning of Worsted in the Workhouse for the Imployment of the Poor there and other poor Inhabitants belonging to the said Parish does not answer the Purpose Intended - but a Disadvantage to the said Parish from the Expense attending the Combing and Dying of the Wool before it is Ready to be spun and Imploying a Spinner on Purpose to Instruct and Superintend the Children Imployed therein and other Incidental Charges attending the same and Whereas the Churchwardens and Overseers of the Poor of the said Parish or a Major Part of them having by a Vestry Order Impowering them so to do Purchased of Mr Wm Laming of Withersden Wool to the Amount of One Hundred Pounds and Borrowed the same for that purpose at lawful interest Now it is hereby Agreed from the Loss already sustained by the said Parish That the above Parish Officers by themselves (or their Agent) shall resell and dispose of the Remainder of the said Wooll now in hand when and so soon as conveniently it may be disposed with the Monies arising therefrom (after deducting Expenses attending the same) to Pay off and Discharge the said Sum of One Hundred Pounds and the Arrears of Interest as far as the same will extend.

In 1789 the overseers made an entry in their account -

> Spent at Flying Horse and King's Head with People that came about the Workhouse
> 2/2d

At no time did the workhouse accommodate more than a small portion of the poor of Wye; most of them remained in their own homes, receiving pensions from the overseers or having their rent paid out of the poor sess. Among these were a number of people with a settlement in Wye, but living in Canterbury or in the neighbouring villages.

It is not easy to assess what life was like in the workhouse. The overseers' accounts record meticulously the expenditure for the poor, but only incidentally show with what degree of harshness or humanity the institution was administered. There was, up and down the country, a growing view that too much was done to make the paupers comfortable, and that giving them pensions to live in their own houses, clothing their children and supplying them with the necessities of life discouraged thrift and put too heavy a burden on the rates. In the course of a century the total of the half yearly poor rate in Wye had risen from £63/17/5d to £482/1/0d.

Knatchbull's Act was widely adopted, but in many cases it led to unhappy results. In Ashford Henry Creed, a local tradesman, urged that the full rigours of the doctrine of "less eligibility" should be applied to the paupers. No relief was to be given for illegitimate children over seven years old, nor for more than three children in one family; the other children were to be taken into the workhouse on the grounds of "the certainty of their being better brought up in a well regulated workhouse than it's possible they can be by a labouring man with so large a family". Vagrants and tramps begging for alms were to be immediately put in the cage and set to beating hemp[1].

In contrast with this draconian regime in Ashford, John Toke, the Squire of Godinton, who was a magistrate, pleaded for a more compassionate approach. He must have known Wye well, as he often "allowed" the Poor Law accounts there. In 1770 he published an anonymous pamphlet (*Five Letters on the State of the Poor in the County of Kent*) in which he wrote - "Most populous Parishes have workhouses which, instead, of being of public utility, are too often the cause of public Distress. For, how often

---

[1] See B. Keith-Lucas, *Parish Affairs* pp. 113-114. In 1818 a "select vestry" was formed in Ashford, which enforced a rigorous regime, reducing the expenditure on weekly relief from £1212 to £358 between 1818 and 1835 (A. J. Pearman, *History of Ashford* (1868) p.140). The Ashford regime was quoted in 1835 by Sir Francis Head as a model for the rest of England. (*Quarterly Review*, Vol LIII, p.473)

does it not happen that some sturdy person is bargained with to take the poor by the lump, who yet is not intended to take them, but to hang over them, like an Egyptian Taskmaster, in terrorem, if they complain to the Justices for want of maintenance."

The treatment of the poor in many parochial workhouses up and down the country became a national scandal. In 1782 a new Poor Law Act (22 Geo.III c.83), known as Gilbert's Act, attempted to deal with this, and in its preamble, referring to Knatchbull's Act, stated that -

> From want of proper regulations and management in the poor-houses or workhouses that have been purchased or hired under the authority of the said Act, and for want of due inspection and control . . . the poor in many places, instead of finding protection and relief, have been much oppressed thereby.

The Act of 1782 was aimed at persuading parishes to group themselves into unions, which would be administered by a board of Guardians, appointed by the Magistrates. The vestrymen of Wye were not in favour of this policy, which would involve the vestry and the overseers losing much of their powers and responsibility, and in 1808 they resolved that Wye should not be incorporated with any other parishes.

It does not appear that the poor in the Workhouse at Wye were ill-treated, but there are hints of mismanagement, as when, in 1771, there is an entry in the Vestry Book -

> Ordered by the Vestry that the 17th Article of the Rules and Orders written in the Workhouse Book be strictly observed and that the Overseers and Guardians for the time being shall see the same duly executed.

There is no evidence of what the 17th Article was, but the implication is that the Master was to exercise a greater degree of authority over the inmates. This assumption is perhaps confirmed by the fact that in April 1765 the vestry

> Agreed to take Thomas Cook's two biggest Boys into the Workhouse (but he refused).

The conflict over how the poor should be treated came to a head in the Commission on the Laws for the Relief of the Poor, whose report, published in 1834, was written by Edwin Chadwick, the leading champion of the doctrine of the "Workhouse Test" and "Less Eligibility". The Commission recommended that the relief of the poor should be taken out of the hands of the local overseers and vestries, and entrusted to the new Boards of Guardians, who would establish the union workhouses. The

Commission's report describes the parish vestries as "the most irresponsible bodies that ever were entrusted with the performance of public duties, or the distribution of public money".

This report led to the passing of the Poor Law Amendment Act of 1834 (4&5 William IV, c.77), establishing the new Poor Law Unions and the much hated union workhouses. It also set up for the first time a central body to supervise the administration of the Poor Law - the Poor Law Commission.

This meant that the vestry no longer had the principal responsibility for the relief of the poor. The Workhouse in Lower Bridge Street was to be sold by the new Poor Law authority - the Guardians of East Ashford Union. But it had been bought with money raised by selling the poor house at Puntowes, which was held as a charity. So, in 1836 the vestry resolved -

> This Vestry finding that about 80 years ago certain premises called Pontowes left by the will of Searles to this parish were sold and the purchase money thereof was applied to the purchase of the above Workhouse it is resolved unanimously that a petition by the Inhabitants of the Parish be presented to the Poor Law Commissioners to allow this parish to take so much of the proceeds of the sale of the workhouse as will replace the purchase money of Pontowes which was so improperly sold to be applied for the charitable purposes originally intended.

After four years of argument with the Guardians the workhouse and the adjoining cottages, which belonged to the parish (Brett's Charity) were finally sold to Thomas Minter of Faversham for £195/5/0d. The vestry spent the money on employing Thomas Thurston of Ashford to make a map of Wye showing the valuation of all the property.

Sickness

Throughout the eighteenth century there was a constant problem of small-pox. Many of the parishioners of Wye died of the infection, and there were few who were never affected. The overseers had to pay out of the poor rate numerous sums for nursing the many victims, and, too often, for their burial. Thus in 1730 Thomas Parker, the overseer, recorded -

Gave Goodwife Kennett in Time of Small Pox	2/0d
Gave them more in illness	5/0d
Pd Goodman Bodkin's ffee for digging the grave and ringing her knell, etc	3/6d
Pd Robert Adman for ordering the buring, myself not having had the small pox	1/0d

In 1742 temporary arrangements were made for the accommodation of parishioners with smallpox and the overseers recorded in their accounts -

Pd Mr Stephen Moor of Hinxhill for a house to put our Small pox people in Nacolt Lane upon contract £1/1/0d

Pd Mrs Philpott for carrying Hunts ffam (family) to Nacolt in time of Small Pox 5/0d

There appears to have been a particularly severe outbreak in 1760 and 1761, and the vestry decided to establish a permanent isolation hospital or "pest house". They needed somewhere outside the thickly populated centre of the village, and decided to take a lease of the White House, which stood in the meadows upstream from the mill and the bridge, beyond what is now Little Chequers. This house stood on the land bequeathed by John Finch of Lympne in 1707 to the Minister, Churchwardens and Overseers of Wye, for the support of five of the eldest and poorest widows of the Parish. So, in 1762 the vestry agreed to pay an annual rent of one pound a year for this house.

Here the Widow Townsend was appointed -

"as soon as it is fitted as a Pest House to take Care of the same and to nurse such Persons as shall be sent thither sick of the Small pox by the officers of the said Parish after the rate of two Shillings by the Week for each Person, and if any of the other Inhabitants of the said Parish shall be sent thither labouring under the same distemper she shall receive and shall not demand more than five Shillings Weekly for her trouble".

This resolution was witnessed by the churchwardens (David Hughes and Valentine Austen), the overseers (Thomas Simpson and John Goldup), John Sawbridge of Olantigh, the Curate (Philip Parsons), Nicholas Brett of Spring Grove, William Allen the schoolmaster, (who wrote the minutes in his excellent script) and seven others.

When the White House had been taken over as a pest house, and duly equipped with furniture, an entry was made in the Poor Book in July 1763-

Paid Mrs Back for wine and Beer had at the White House for the Small Pox	4/6d
More	4d

It appears that small pox continued to be a major problem for many years. In 1776 the overseer's account included these entries -

pd for Potatoes and aples for the poor during the small pox	5/0d
Mr Scudamore[1] for Inoculating the Poor being 39 Persons at 5/3d each	£10/4/9d
Ditto, another bill	£2/8/9d
Mr Willis for Inoculations 16	£4/4/0d
Pd Terry for Fowler's Housekeeper and Child during the Small Pox	10/0d
Paid more for Fowler's Housekeeper	7/0d
Paid for Carrying Mrs Maxted to the Whitehouse during the Smallpox	2/0d
Paid Mr Terry for Mrs Maxted at the Whitehouse during the Smallpox	10/0d

On the 1st of July, 1781 the vestry decided -

to give Wm Scott of Naccolt Lanes in Wye Parish one Guinea to support himself Wife and three Children having been ill for some time.

Three weeks later they agreed -

to give Wm Scott the further Sum of ten shillings and sixpence he continuing very ill - also to be at the expense of inoculating Richard Ambrose Wife and Family (who live at Harrietsham) for the Small Pox and that one of the Parish Officers is required to go to see after them forthwith - also to Give John Kennett who lives at Cucklescomb one shirt.

This was signed by the overseers and the churchwardens and by William Scudamore, the parish doctor.

The Poor Book (or overseers' account book) shows that one of the Wye overseers then rode over to Harrietsham to make the arrangements, and paid £2/5/0d for the inoculation of Richard Ambrose and his six children. As their settlement was in Wye, this parish had not only to pay for the

---

[1] William Scudamore was the parish doctor. Vaccination had not yet been introduced, as Jenner did not disclose his discovery until 1798. Before that a system of inoculation had been used, based on experience in Turkey.

inoculation, but also to support the family thereafter at a rate of 10/0d a week. There were also incidental expenses for travelling to Harrietsham and reimbursing the expenditure of the overseers of Harrietsham. The vestry accordingly resolved to pay Richard Ambrose's rent, "he and his wife being very old and sickly". The vestry had been generous to the Ambrose family in previous years; in 1776 they had -

> agreed to Lend Richard Ambrose a parishioner of this Parish, Shoemaker, the sum, of fifteen pounds to set him up at his trade in the Parish of Harrietsham in Kent afore-said.

They had also employed Richard Coleman, a local attorney, to recover a legacy left to his wife, Anne, but which she had never received.

Occasionally the expense of hospital treatment for a parishioner had to be met out of the overseer's funds. In April 1779 the vestry resolved that -

> It is agreed that John, the son of the Widow Moss of this Parish being very Lame, to be at the Expense of sending him up to Saint Thomas Hospital and not being able to go without his Mother have also agreed to be at the Expense for her to Go with him.

The overseers accordingly gave her £1/1/0d for her expenses, but the arrangement for the admission of John Moss seems to have misfired. A kind friend of his mother's came to the rescue, and wrote to the authorities in Wye -

> May 2nd 1779, London
>
> Gentlemen this is to Acquaint you that Mrs Mosse came to London with an intent to get her son into the Hospital, but her Letter which she had from Esqr Sawbridge failing she knowing of me Beg'd my Assistance she being an Utter Stranger in London. I Lent her all the Assistance in my power which got him in, & gave Security for him- the expense in the Hospital will be 4 pence per day, and 3d per week washing which I shall Discharge. If he Dies they will send to me to Bury him or when he comes out I shall Defray the Expenses and send the Account Over,
>
> I am your most Obedt
> and Hum. Serv.
> Jno May.
>
> Master of the Sheerness Hoy.[1]

The next entry in the overseer's accounts is -

Boy's Hospital Bill   £1/15/4d

---

[1] A hoy was a small sailing ship, plying between London and the Kent Coast, carrying goods and pas-sengers.

Churchwardens

Beatrice and Sidney Webb, writing about the constitution and functions of the parish in English villages, said that "At the close of the seventeenth century the student will discern few parishes alike in their constitution. The customary and statutory powers and obligations are found, as a matter of fact, divided in confused and inextricable ways among all the different functionaries and dignitaries - among the Churchwardens, Surveyors of Highways, and Overseers of the Poor on the one hand; and on the other, among the Lord of the Manor, his Steward and other officers, the Incumbent and the Archdeacon, and the Justices of the Peace in their individual capacities or sitting in Petty Sessions or Quarter Sessions".[1]

The churchwardens, like the vestry in which they played a leading part, were not established by statute, but evolved out of common law. They were elected by the vestry, and a number of statutes and legal decisions defined the people who were exempt from being elected - barristers, apothecaries, dissenting clergy, convicted felons and militiamen.

Their primary duty was to maintain the parish church and to levy a rate or Sess for that purpose. They were *ex-officio* overseers of the poor. They had a duty to enforce some varied aspects of the law, such as the statutes forbidding sports on Sunday and such offences as drunkenness, false weights and measures, tracing hares in the snow[2], selling corn by wrong measure, eating flesh on fish days, and enforcing the laws about burial in wool. They were responsible for paying the rewards to parishioners who killed the vermin of the countryside - foxes, badgers, stoats, hedgehogs, sparrows and polecats.[3]

Whatever may have been the legal position, it is clear that the more important decisions about the structure and furnishing of the church were taken not by the churchwardens alone, but by the vestry, of which the churchwardens were members, regularly attending the meetings.

---

[1] *The Parish and the County*, p.6.

[2] Under the statute 1 James I, c.27 "any person who shall course any hares in the snow shall on conviction be committed to gaol for three months unless he pay the churchwardens for the use of the poor 20s for every hare".

[3] In 1727 the churchwardens of Wye paid for 84 hedgehogs, 8 foxes, and one polecat. In 1684 they had paid for 31 hedgehogs, 2 foxes, 60 rooks, 1 buzzard, 12 crows and 69 daws. In 1802 they paid for 148 sparrows, 10 foxes and one badger.

Unfortunately the churchwarden's accounts for the period 1692 to 1728 are missing, and no vestry minutes survive from before 1724. So it is that there are no records of the discussions about the rebuilding of the church tower after it had suddenly collapsed in 1686; the rebuilding was not started until 1702.

The minute books of 1724 and subsequent years show the vestry deciding matters of minor importance, such as the appointment of an assistant sexton and the allocation of the pews in the church. Thus on the 1st November in that year they decided that -

> John Weller, John Hudson, Widow Back, her son, etc should have the two pews next adjoining Esquire Johnson's Servant Maids Pew (which is the third Pew on the left hand of the entrance on coming in at the South Door entering the second Space) the other two Leading on the Left hand from that to the West Door in Lieu of two Pews fronting on the Chancell on the Right and Left hands, etc.

In 1730 the vestry authorised Stephen Bowyer to erect at his own cost a gallery in the South aisle of the church, to be 35 ft by 13 ft, and he was authorised to let or sell the pews in this gallery to his own profit.

In December 1780 the vestry -

> Ordered and directed that the Churchwardens of this Parish shall Clear the Singing Gallery of all such Persons who shall not enter into Articles to Sing in Four Parts - the Singing Gallery being erected and appointed for the accommodation of the Singers only and not for any other Persons Except the Churchwardens and Overseers.

On the 30th January, 1781, the vestry authorised the building of another gallery along the South wall of the church. It was specified that when built this gallery was to be used by William Scudamore, the parish doctor, William Kennett of Wye Court and five other members of the vestry, 'exclusive of all other persons'.

The church bells gave the churchwardens and the vestry very considerable trouble; on the 27th January, 1733 the Vestry resolved that -

> The Treble Bell should be taken down and sent to London to Mr Phelps to cast two others by, in order to our Peale of eight Bells etc.

A week later the vestry considered the matter again, and ordered that -

> the Churchwardens shall contract to alter the Frame and new hang the Bells with two new ones with Such Persons as is willing to undertake to doe the same in the best manner and at the cheapest rate.

Forty years later they decided that all the bells should be replaced. On the 2nd of August, 1774, the vestry -

Agreed to have eight new bells, the Tenor to weigh twenty two hundred weight and the rest in Proportion the whole Peal to weigh eighty eight hundred Weight a little more or less - at 13 pence per pound - the Bells that are now in the Steeple the Bellfounders to take at an equal weight of Metal with the new Bells at the rate of 19d per Pound . . . and to allow the Bellhanger according to an Estimate Delivered in £35/12/0d.

Later that year they decided -

that a Ringing Loft in the Steeple of the said Parish Church shall be immediately Erected by David Hughes Robt Elliott & John Batchellor Carpenters and to allow them for Erecting and Building the same the Sum of Twenty Pounds (exclusive of Bricklayers and Masons work) & Also Exclusive of a Doorcase and Door entering into the said Loft.

In March, 1778 they decided that the interior of the church needed to be whitewashed, and the interior of the roof plastered -

It was then agreed to Ceile the Isles of the said Parish Church and to allow Will'm Allen Sen'r and Will'm Allen Jun'r ten Pence a Yard for Workmanship only Beer included . . . The Carpenters to find an Equal Share of Good Hard Lathes and every other Article that is wanting in their Business - At all Day work each man is to be allowed three pence a Day for Beer.

The Churchwardens were legally overseers of the poor, in addition to those so appointed specifically as overseers by the vestry, but they generally left such business as relieving the poor, running the workhouse and pursuing the fathers of bastard children to the annually appointed overseers. They did, however, often pay small sums to strangers travelling through the parish, to help them on their way. Some of these were soldiers or sailors travelling with a pass, but in 1738 there was a peculiar entry in the churchwarden's accounts -

Item, gave to an innumerable many Seamen with passes Slaves from Turkey with their Tongues cut out and other people Losses by Fire etc.   £2/11/6d

There are two entries, both in 1770, recording that Mrs Beale and Mrs Part each paid 6/8d "for breaking up the Church". It appears that they were both widows, and that their husbands, John Beale, a surgeon, and John Part, a weaver, both died in 1770 and were buried under the stone floor of the nave of the church. So this was a fee charged for breaking up the stone paving of the church.

One function of the churchwardens was to record the exact boundaries of the parish - important because the sesses were based on the occupation of land, and also because one's settlement commonly depended on the parish in which one was born. The Wye churchwardens decided in 1743 to survey and record the boundaries of the parish. Fortunately there was among the inhabitants of the village a man, Michael Moon, who was an expert cartographer. He made several maps of the parish, including one of the King's Wood (then owned by the Earl of Winchilsea and Nottingham), one of the Whitehouse land, one of the "Laines" (the open fields in Wye, Godmersham and Crundal). He also drew the "Road Map" of Wye which was made in 1763 in order to assess the length of highway under the control of the parochial surveyor and that under the control of the Turnpike Trustees, under the Turnpike Act of 1761[1].

On November the 14th, 1743, Thomas Franklin, the Churchwarden, recorded in his accounts -

Pd Mich. Moon for going the Bounds of the Parish, through the Earl of Rockingham's Wood etc.	7/6d
Pd him more for a Map with the Bounds	10/6d
Pd Goodman Hogbin, for going at the same time	1/6d
Pd Mr Warham on the same	4/0d
Pd Mr Wm Kennett and the two Churchwardens each on the same account	1/0d

Again in 1746 there is another entry on the same matter -

Pd Mich. Moon for going part of the Bounds of the Parish against Brabourne	1/0d

The churchwardens had to provide for some functions more directly related to the church. For example, in 1744 the first items in the account were -

Spent at the Visitation	£1/19/6d
Pd for Swearing etc	2/0d
Pd for Bread Cheese Beer for the Children that went to be confirmed	5/6d
Pd the Sexton for going with them	1/0d
Pd the Minister's dinner dining with the Bishop	5/0d

---

[1] Copies of these four maps are included in the portfolio of maps compiled by the Wye Historical Society in 1984. Michael Moon was the son of the shoemaker, also Michael Moon.

Wye Charities

With the dissolution of the Monasteries and the Protestant revolution under Henry VIII a great impetus was given to the establishment by will of local charities for the relief of the poor. No longer did testators leave their property to pay for the saying of masses for their souls, and no longer did the monasteries provide relief for the poor, the aged and the disabled.

In the next two centuries there were founded, up and down the country, thousands of local charities, endowed by pious benefactors with the rent of land, or with rent charges arising out of land.[1] In Wye there already existed the College, founded by Cardinal Kemp in 1431-2, as a corporate body of secular priests, with a grammar school attached. These were princely bene-factions, given by a great Prince of the Church, Lord Chancellor of England, Archbishop of Canterbury, and Cardinal Bishop of Santa Rufina.

The humbler squires and farmers of Wye and its neighbourhood thought in less magnificent terms, but none the less several of them founded chari-ties in Wye which still, in altered forms, survive today.

(1) Finch's Charity

In 1707 John Finch of Lympne bequeathed his estates in Thanet, Wye, Godmersham, and Crundale, for the relief of the poor. Most of the land was, by the terms of the will, subject to life interests for members of Finch's family, so the trustees could not distribute the rents until the life tenants died, or the parish bought their interests.

The will was long and elaborate, but the essential elements were -

a) 105 acres of farmland in St. Nicholas at Wade in Thanet were bequeathed to the churchwardens and overseers of St. Nicholas and of Wye. The revenue from this was to be given to eight poor men in each parish, provided that they had never received parish relief.

b) 46 acres in Wye (the White House Land sometimes referred to as Widows' Land) to the churchwardens and overseers of Wye, the revenue to be distributed to five elderly widows who had never received parochial relief.

---

[1] A rent is payment to the owner of land for the right to use it; a rent-charge is a payment by the owner of the land of a fixed amount, charged on the land.

c) Land in Bilting (36 acres) and in Wye, Godmersham and Crundale and six "cowshares" in the "laines"[1] together with the adjoining meadow called Temple Hope, bequeathed to the Ministers of Wye and Godmersham, the income from which was to be given to six of the oldest and poorest of Wye and of Godmersham and two of Crundale, who had never received parish relief.

d) The will provided that if at any time the trustees for any of the parishes should "alter or contradict my will or misapply or divert the said rents and profits to any other use" the property was to pass to the trustees of the other parishes.

e) The distribution was to be limited to members of the Church of England.

After the death of John Finch there were disputes and lawsuits about the will, and the vestry appointed John Sawbridge, Robert Warham and William and Robert Dann to conduct the case on behalf of the parish. The vestry also decided to buy out the life interest of John Finch's family. William Kennett of Wye Court became the tenant of the White House Land at a rent of £60 a year, but the White House itself was rented from him for use as an isolation hospital or pest house.

So the rents, less the outgoings, and expenses were duly distributed by the churchwardens and overseers to five widows, and a share of the revenue from the farm at St Nicholas at Wade was distributed to eight poor men. There was however apparently some difficulty in finding eight elderly and deserving parishioners who had never received parish relief, but who were in need. Comparison of the lists of the people to whom these doles were given with the valuation list for the poor sess shows that a number of them were occupiers of substantial properties, and were presumably not in urgent need. In some years the money was distributed to only five or six people, not to eight, as directed in Finch's will. Perhaps the trustees could not find enough candidates. Many of those to whom the money was given lived not in Wye but in other villages in the neighbourhood, but presumably they had their settlements in Wye.

There was usually an item in the accounts for four or five shillings for "Expenses at Distributing at the King's Head" or at the Flying Horse. In 1788 the accounts show that the expenses at distributing to five widows

---

[1] A cowshare was the right to pasture a cow in the open field called "the Laines", lying downstream from Olantigh. These rights were attached to individual farms in the three parishes.

amounted to 9/4d. When the churchwardens of Wye went to Canterbury to meet the "Island Gentlemen" (that is, the tenants of the land at St Nicholas at Wade) to collect the rent there is an entry in the accounts -

> Journey to Canterbury to Receive the Rent as Usual (a Bottle Wine for the Tenant and Self Included) 7/6d

The land at Bilting was bought by the overseers in 1772. From the year 1785, when the tenancy of the land passed to John Clifford, there was a deduction every half year of six shillings for "A Cow Share Deducted".

(2) Dryland's Charity

In 1606 Richard Dryland of Wye gave to the poor of Wye two acres in the King's Wood, to be used to supply the poor with firewood. The overseer's accounts contain numerous references to this, such as one in 1789 -

> For Wood Brought from the Wood belonging to the Poor of Wye £3/15/6d

And in 1792 -

> Nic Swaine for 1/2 Load of Wood for Ja. Quested 8/0d
> Do. for 1/2 Load for John Lawrence 8/0d
> Do. for 1 Load for Thos Wilds 15/0d

The boundaries of the two acres referred to are clearly shown on a map made in 1762 by Michael Moon, the surveyor who lived in Wye. But even so it seems that it was not always easy to identify the land. In 1795 the Churchwarden, Thomas Quested, recorded

> Feb. 8. Going to Look at the Wood belonging to the Poor of Wye in the Virgin Wood 1/-
> Gave George Epps for going to Show me the Wood 1/-

So also today it is difficult to identify this particular plot.

(3) Cole's Charity

In 1653, four years after the execution of Charles I in Whitehall, Robert Cole of Wye gave by deed a sum of £100 to trustees who were to pay two pounds a year to the parson to preach two sermons in Wye Church annually on the 30th of January. The balance of the income was to be distributed to the poor in loaves of bread. The money was invested by the trustees in land in the parish of Brabourne, but this was later sold, and the gift to the poor was merged into the Wye Almshouse Charity; the payment for the sermon still continues, but has not increased with inflation.

Little is known about Mr Cole, except that he died in 1663 "beyond London", and his body was brought back to Wye to be buried beside his wife, who was the sister of Colonel Richard Thornhill of Olantigh. Colonel Thornhill was an ardent Royalist, who had ridden out of Wye with a troop of horse which he had recruited at his own expense, to join King Charles when he raised his standard at Nottingham in 1639. He was the husband of Lady Joanna Thornhill, the founder of the school in Wye.

The date on which the sermons were to be preached is significant - the 30th January is the anniversary of the death of King Charles. By the Royalists it was regarded as a day of national mourning for "Charles, King and Martyr". But perhaps more significant is the theme of the texts from which Mr Cole decreed the sermon should be preached. Eight texts from the Old Testament were designated, and these had all a common theme - the wickedness of those who lift up their hands against an annointed king. Among these texts are -

> Lamentations, Chap. V, v. 15 and 16; "The Joy of our hearts is ceased; our dance is turned into mourning. The Crown is fallen from our head; woe unto us, that we have sinned".
>
> Micah, Chap. IV. v.9; "now why dost thou cry out aloud? Is there no king in thee? Is thy counsellor perished? For pangs have taken thee as a woman in travail"
>
> I Samuel Chap.XXVI v. 9; "David said to Abishai Destroy him not, for who can stretch forth his hand against the Lord's annointed, and be guiltless?".

Clearly the parson was to preach a Royalist sermon, bewailing the execution of the King, even though there might be some risk in doing this while Cromwell was in power. But Mr Cole had fixed on him the duty to do so. Whether Cole himself proclaimed his Royalist sympathies we do not know. It may be that he rode with his brother-in-law to join the royal forces in Nottingham.

It appears that the Curate did preach the sermon every year, and the relevant entry was made in the accounts -

The Revd Mr Parsons preaching two sermons 30th Jan	£2/0/0d
The Clerk Cleaning a Monument	4/0d
Lawrence Austen for Bread[1]	£1/5/2d
Quit Rent	2/10d
Spent at Receiving Rent	2/0d

[1] It would appear that Lawrence Austen was a baker.

From 1772 the entry was changed, to read -

The Clerk for not cleaning the monument[1]	4/0d

After two more years the mention of the monument no longer appears. There is then another entry under the heading of "Mr Cole's Legacy" -

Mr David Hughes for measuring the Timber	2/0d
Thos Terry for Felling Timber and making Faggots and Cordwood	7/0d
George Allen, Carpenter	£1/0/2d

The relevance of this is not apparent, as the purpose of the charity was for preaching a sermon, and any surplus to be given to the poor in the form of bread.

(4) Searles Hospital

The houses left by Robert Searles for the poor of Wye, called Puntowes (see page 38)

(5) "The Widows Suits" or Carkeridge's Charity

In 1640 Thomas Carkeridge of Maidstone gave by will a rent charge on land at Bilting and Godmersham to provide clothes for four poor widows. This was regularly distributed, not in money but in cloth, purchased by the churchwardens for the purpose. The description of the clothes was exactly defined in the will. In 1744 when Thomas Jarman and James Kennett were the overseers, there is an entry "but could not find who had the suits", and in 1748, 1752 and 1756 there are entries "who had the Suits I know not who".

(6) Brett's Charity

William Brett of Kennington gave a rent charge of one pound a year out of a house near the workhouse in Bridge Street, to clothe a poor boy. The house was later bought by the parish for poor families.

There is no further reference to the express purpose of the bequest, but as the overseers did regularly spend money on the clothing of poor boys, there was no real breach of trust.

---

[1] See Hubbard, *The Old Book of Wye* p.160. It appears that the monument in question was that of Elizabeth, wife of the testator. The monument was destroyed when the church tower collapsed in 1686.

(7) Lady Joanna Thornhill's Charity

In addition to her benefaction to found a school which still bears her name, Lady Joanna, who died in 1708, gave by her will two pounds a year to the Curate of Wye to preach a sermon on Good Friday, and thirty shillings a year for three poor men and three poor women, who were to attend the church when the sermon was preached. The remainder was to be spent on bread to be distributed on Easter day. She also left £500 for poor householders of Wye, which was invested in the purchase of 35 acres of farmland at Sevington. Of the school that she founded Edward Hasted wrote in 1798 -

> This beneficial institution, so greatly to the advantage of this parish, is in a very flourishing state, there being at present more than one hundred boys and girls taught in it.
>
> The master of the English boys school has a salary of thirty pounds per annum, for which he is to teach every poor boy in the parish reading, writing and arithmetic, from the age of eight years to twelve. The mistress of the girls school has twenty pounds per annum, for which she is to instruct every poor girl in the parish in reading and needlework, and they are to attend the master of the boys school two hours in the day, to be taught to write.

(8) Morris' Charity

In 1612 William Morris gave by his will two pounds a year, charged on land at Naccolt. This was to be distributed annually by the churchwardens in sums of two shillings to each of twenty parishioners.

(9) Sir George Wheler's Bequest

The original statutes of Wye College provided that it should include a grammar school, providing free education for the boys of Wye. When Henry VIII dissolved the monasteries (including Wye College), the property of the College vested in the Crown, but provision was made for the continuance of the grammar school, the salary of the headmaster being paid out of the rent of the land. The property passed through the hands of a succession of owners, including Sir George Wheler who was born in 1650 at Breda, where his parents, who were Royalists, were in exile. He was then educated at Wye Grammar School and Lincoln College, Oxford. He and his son founded a scholarship to that College, for boys educated in Wye, which has been lost through non-use. He was a Canon of Durham Cathedral and married to a niece of Lady Thornhill. In 1724 he bequeathed the College buildings to trustees (including John Sawbridge) to house both the Grammar School and Lady Joanna Thornhill's school.

An undated paper in an early nineteenth century hand writing, kept at Wye College with the vestry books, etc., records that -

> Sir George Wheler's appointment of the College - The Master of the male Children shall have the great Hall to teach the male Children in. And further the said Master shall have for Habitation, lodging and other convenience, the Wainscott Ground Room, in the West and North corner of the house next to the Church yard west, and to work the Garden North, with the Chambers over them to the great stair case, which shall be in common for the use of both Master and Mistress of the said Charity Children.

> The Mistress of the said Charity female Children shall have the great Wainscott Room called the Great Parlour lying and being Situated at the North end of the Great Hall, and extending to the great stair case, to teach the Charity female Children in, and all the Rooms, or Chambers over it unto the Great Stair Case above and below for her Lodging and other convenience.

Another paper with this, but apparently written in the 18th Century, records that "Sir George Wheler Kt left, by his last Will, bearing date 1713, the College of Wye and Appurtenances, as an augmentation to Lady Joanna Thornhill's Charity viz he left the above for the uses following, The half of the College with the Garden next the Street to the Use of the Grammar Master, & the other half with the rest of the appurtenances as an augmentation to Lady Joanna Thornhill's Charity." Hasted, writing in the late eighteenth century, notes that the school room is an old stone building of about the time of the college's foundation. The building "now makes a very handsome appearance having been recently repaired by the trustees".

(10) Jarman's Fields

William Jarman (or German) bequeathed in 1479 the land called the Cherry Orchard (now called Jarman's Field), the rent to be used for the repair of the church. Hasted records that in his time the field was let for £2/10/0d per annum. A few years ago it was sold for development for a quarter of a million pounds.

(11) Kemp's Almshouse

Sir Thomas Kemp of Olantigh, established before 1562 an Almshouse on Bolt's Hill, where the Almshouses still stand, serving their original purpose.

In addition to these charitable foundations and to the educational trusts established by Lady Joanna Thornhill and Sir George Wheler, there were numerous bequests of money or property for the benefit of the poor of Wye.

It appears that towards the end of 18th and in the early years of the 19th century there was some degree of laxity in the administration of the parochial charities. In 1837 there were no living trustees of the charities established by Thomas Kipps, Thomas Carkeridge, William Morris and Richard Hawke. In 1863 on the application of the Vicar, Churchwardens and Overseers a scheme was made by the Charity Commissioners, to establish a system of joint administration, with a single body of trustees. This covered the charities founded by Finch, Morris, Kipps, Carkeridge, Cole, Tylden, Wood, Brett, Hawke, Kemp and Cook. They are now merged into the single Almshouse Trust.

In many of these cases the testator left in his will a charge to be paid out of the profits of a specified piece of land. The amount was fixed in terms of pounds and shillings. In the course of two or three centuries the value of these fixed charges has been dramatically reduced. Inflation has reduced them until they are scarcely worth collecting. In other cases, where the land itself was bequeathed, the Charity Commissioners favoured a policy in the 19th century of selling the land and investing the proceeds in the 3% government stock. This has also proved to be an unfortunate policy. On the other hand charities such as Jarman's, which owned land suitable for development have grown much richer.

The Highways

The roads of Wye parish in the 18th century were in a bad state. Edward Hasted, writing towards the end of the century, probably advised by Nicholas Brett, stated that the whole of the village was unpaved, and the "Town Map" of 1746 shows several springs in Bridge Street, running down to the river. This caused the houses there to be built above street level, with steps up to the front door. Other streets were not much better, and a number of the older houses still have shoescrapers by their doors, because of the mud in the road.

Responsibility for the highways was vested in the surveyors of highways. Under a series of Acts from 1555 to 1766 surveyors were appointed every year. The constables, church wardens and inhabitants were to meet once a year and compile a list of the inhabitants who were eligible for the appointment. The qualification was the ownership of land worth £10 a year or personal property worth £100.[1] This list was passed to the Justices who chose from it the names of two or three who were to serve as surveyors of highways. The vestrymen did not always comply exactly with the law, and it was nobody's duty to make them do so. Until 1767 they did not submit a list of qualified people to the Justices, but themselves appointed or nominated two or three parishioners to serve as surveyors for the ensuing year (including in 1764, '65 and '66 John Sawbridge of Olantigh).

The Act provided that if the constables, churchwardens and surveyors failed to return the list of qualified parishioners they were each to forfeit one pound (half to the informer, half to the repair of the highways). There is however no record of any such penalty being collected. In 1770 they did for the first time submit a list, and thereafter they complied with the law.

The surveyors were responsible for keeping the roads in repair, and they were empowered to call out the able bodied men of the parish to work on them for six days each year - a duty known as "Statute Labour". Those who owned horses and carts were to bring them to help by carrying the stones

---

[1] In 1773 four out of ten names submitted were members of the Kennett family, the principal farmers of the parish.

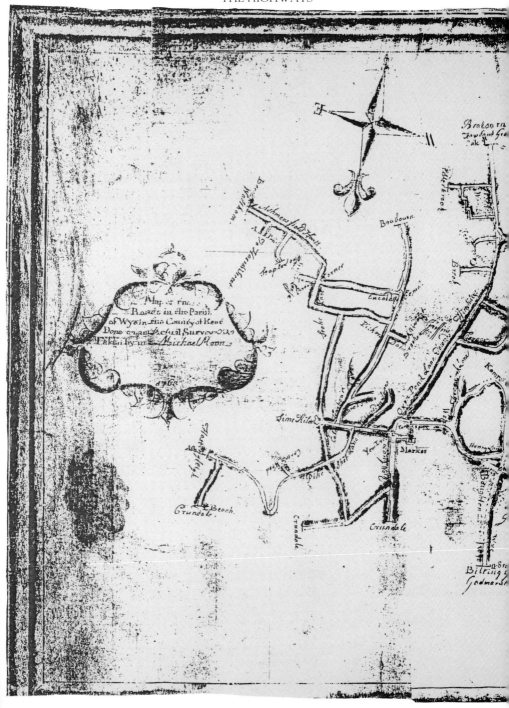

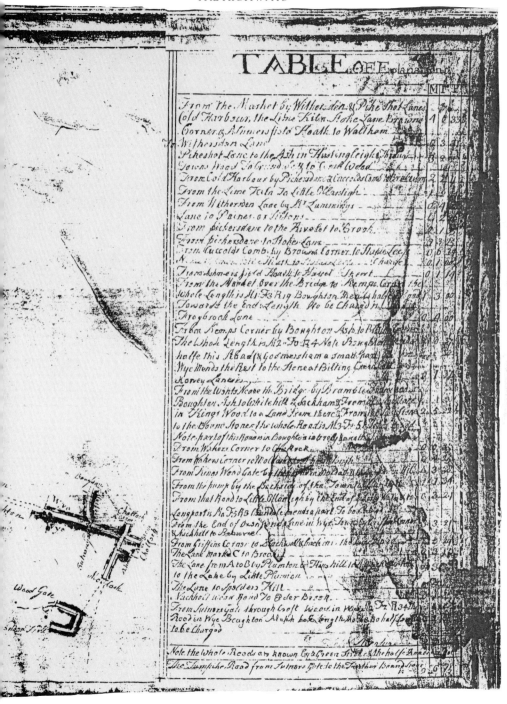

for making up the roads, and it was a common practice for the surveyors to pay the children to collect the stones in the fields. It was open to those liable for statute duty to pay instead an annual fee or composition. This was not a flat rate, but was based on the valuations made for the poor sess, and was charged not only on the residents in the parish, but on all those who were occupiers of land in the parish - including the "Outdwellers".

Instead of relying on the "statute labour" the surveyors spent the composition money on hiring labourers from the parish, on the hire of horses and carts, and on "pence money" for the children.

In 1736 the vestry authorised the surveyors to borrow the money to make Stocks Lane (Scotton Street) and the road over Wye Down into "a good passable Coach Road". From time to time authority was granted to the surveyors to borrow money for other improvements, and in 1782 it was decided to make a contract with John Sawbridge, despite the fact that, as a Member of Parliament and an Alderman of the City of London, he cannot have had much time for the parish affairs of Wye. It was then agreed that -

> John Sawbridge is at his own cost and charge to repair and keep repaired the High Road leading from a certain place called the Yew Tree[1] to Olantigh and a certain High Road leading from a place called Cold Harbour to Little Olantigh and the High Road leading from a certain place called Courtfield Gate up the Downs as far as the Gate at the entrance of the Lane joining to Mr Swan's House in Hastingleigh Parish and as far as the Gate off the Downs leading to Pet Street, in consideration whereof the said John Sawbridge is excused doing any Statute Duty in the Highways of this Parish or paying any composition for the same.

A similar agreement was made with regard to the road to Waltham -

> Agreed that Gibbs of Ashenfield Farm in the parish of Waltham shall keep in good repair at his own Cost & Charge the road upon Ashenfield Heath and also the Road leading from the same Heath towards Waltham (and lying in Wye Parish) Allowing him for the same fourteen Shillings per Annum by the Surveyors of Wye Parish for the time being.

There is no evidence that any actual statute labour was performed, at least in the latter part of the century. The earliest surviving account book, started in 1827[2] shows no sign of statute labour, but long lists of the parishioners who paid the composition.

Despite the efforts of the surveyors of highways up and down the country, the country roads, in the early eighteenth century, were in a very bad

---

[1] i.e. "Golden Square", the cross roads at the junction of Olantigh Road, Scotton Street, Upper Bridge Street and the High Street.

[2] The earlier surveyor's account books had been destroyed in 1854.

condition. Hasted, writing of a parish near Ashford, stated that the roads there "are hardly passable after any rain, being so miry that the traveller's horse frequently plunges through them up to the girth of the saddle, and the wagons sinking so deep in the ruts, as to slide along on the nave of the wheels and axle of them".[1]

It was the state of the parish highways in many parts of England that led in the latter part of the century to a series of petitions to Parliament for the establishment of a more efficient system - the turnpike trusts, administered by groups of squires, parsons and professional men, and financed by tolls charged on all vehicles using the roads. Forty nine such turnpike trusts were set up in Kent, including one established under an Act passed in 1761 for "amending the Road from Faversham by Bacon's Water through Ashford to Hythe, and from Bacon's Water to Holy Lane in Wincheap near the City of Canterbury", which passed through part of the parish of Wye.

The preamble to this Act declared that -

> Whereas the road leading out of the great Post Road near the Town of Faversham over Boughton Leeze and Kennington Leeze by a Place called Bacon's Water in the Parish of Kennington to Kemp's Corner in the Parish of Boughton Aluph and from there by a Place Called Bilting through the parishes of Godmersham in the County of Kent to a certain Lane called Holy Lane in Wincheap near the City of Canterbury are by means of great Traffic in a ruinous Condition and in certain parts so narrow and incommodious that Waggons and other Carriages cannot pass by each other.

A body of 125 trustees was appointed by the Act. These included a number of the squires and other important people living in or around Wye - Sir Wyndham Knatchbull, Sir John Honywood, Sir Brook Bridges, William Deedes, Thomas Knight, John Sawbridge, Jacob Sawbridge, John Elias Sawbridge, John and Nicholas Toke, and Nicholas Brett.

Toll gates were set up, with toll houses beside them - one at Kemp's Corner, which is still standing. Here the tolls were to be collected; one penny for a single horse, sixpence for a carriage with two horses, one shilling and six pence for a vehicle with six horses, and ten shillings for hauling or drawing timber along the surface of the road. Under an Act of 1753[2] (which, later in the century, was extended and elaborated) no wagon or cart was allowed on the turnpike road unless the fellies of the wheels were at least nine inches wide, thus serving to roll the surface of the road, rather than make deep ruts in it.

---

[1] Vol VII, p.221

[2] 26, George. II, c.30

One problem that arose was the apportionment of the statute labour or the composition money between the turnpike road and the other parish roads under the management of the surveyor of highways. In order to calculate this the vestry employed Michael Moon, a resident in the village, to draw up a detailed map[1] from which this could be calculated.

Commercially the turnpike trust was not a success. By 1835 the total annual income was £1898/18/8d. Of this £230/15/9d was spent on manual labour (there was no statute labour performed) and £209/2/1d on team labour (horses and carts), but £405 was spent on paying the interest on the accumulated debts, which amounted to £8530/6/0d.[2] By this time the railways were beginning to threaten the survival of the turnpikes.

The turnpike from the top of Charing Hill to Chilham was established by an Act of 1809. It ran for a short distance through a detached part of Wye parish at Challock, and so the Wye surveyors of highways had to make a small contribution to the trustees, in lieu of statute labour. From Charing Hill to Challock this was a new road, driven through the Longbeech Woods, which were owned partly by the See of Canterbury and partly by the Dering family. Toll gates were set up at Chilham and at Challock.

---

[1] The original is among the Parish Council papers in the College Library.
[2] Abstract of the General Statements of the Several Turnpike Trusts, 1837.

The End of the Vestry

In the latter part of the 18th century the parish vestry was the ruler of the village. It was, however, not completely independant. In a number of ways it was controlled by the Justices - they chose the surveyors, the overseers, the surveyors of highways and the constables, and they had to approve the parish accounts. In these ways, both in Quarter Sessions and individually, they were in strict law the rulers of rural England, but in practice it was the parish vestries and the parish officers who made the day to day decisions, and got them formally confirmed by the Justices, or, in many cases, forgot to get them confirmed.

Bit by bit many of the functions of the vestry were transferred by statute to other, newly created bodies (the Quangos of two centuries ago). More and more the parishes united to pass their Poor Law functions to new unions under local acts or under Gilbert's Act of 1782, until the Poor Law Act of 1834 established the pattern of Unions and Workhouses over the whole country. So too control of the major highways passed by Local Acts to the turnpike trusts, and later many of the lesser roads were transferred under the Highways Act of 1862 to the new Highways Boards. Since the passing of the Local Government Act, 1894, all highways have been the responsibility of either the County or the District Council. The Public Health Act of 1848 establised Local Boards of Health, taking over some of the other functions of the vestries.

The creation of County Councils in 1888 and of Rural District Councils in 1894 further reduced the range of activities of the vestries, and finally by the Local Government Act of 1894 there were transferred to the new Parish Councils all the remaining civil functions of the parish vestries. The vestries survived, but with no functions except in relation to the Church. In 1922 the Parochial Church Councils (Powers) Measure tranferred the remaining functions to the new Parochial Church Councils, leaving the vestries with only one power - the appointment of the churchwardens and sidesmen at the annual Easter Vestry.

Bibliography

Archbold, J.F.,	The Justice of the Peace and Parish	
	Officer, 3vols.	(1842)
Berry, William,	County Genealogies - Kent	(1830)
Brabourne, Lord,	Letters of Jane Austen	(1884)
Brayley, E.W.,	The Beauties of England and Wales,	
	Vol. VIII	(1808)
Burn, Richard,	The Justice of the Peace and Parish	
	Officer, 10th edn.	(1766)
Ditchfield, G.M.and		
Keith-Lucas, Bryan,	A Kentish Parson	(1991)
Furley, Robert,	A History of the Weald of Kent,	
	3 Vols.	(1871)
"Gentleman of the	The New Parish Officer,	
Middle Temple,"	2nd edn	(1767)
Gentleman's Magazine,		
Glasscock, H.H.,	Article in *Wye Local History* Spring 1984	
	"Social Services in Wye in the 1700's"	
Hasted, Edward,	The History and Topographical Survey of the	
	County of Kent, 1st edn,	(1778-1799)
	2nd edn	(1797-1801)
Hill, Bridget	The Republican Virago	(1993)
History of Parliament,	The Commons	
Hubbard, G.E.,	The Old Book of Wye	(1951)
Ingram Hill, D.,	The Six Preachers of Canterbury Cathedral,	(1982)
Keith-Lucas, Bryan,	Parish Affairs-the Government of Kent under	
	George III	(1986)
Knatchbull-Hugesson,		
Sir Hughe	Kentish Family	(1960)
Lane, M.,	Jane Austen's Family	(1984)
Morris, W.S.,	The History and Topography of Wye	(1842)
Nicholls, Sir	A History of the English Poor Law.	
George, & Mackay,	3 Vols	(1899 and 1904)
Thomas,		
Orwin, C.E. &	A History of Wye Church and Wye	
Williams, S.,	College	(1913)
Pearce, Thomas,	The Complete Justice of the Peace and Parish	
	Officer	(1756)

BIBLIOGRAPHY

Pearman, A.J.,	History of Ashford	(1868)
Report of the Royal Commission on the Poor Laws		(1834)
Ruderman, Arthur	A History of Ashford	(1994)
Seymour, Charles,	New Topographical Historical and Commercial Survey of the Cities, Towns and Villages of the County of Kent	(1776)
Smith, John Russell,	Bibliotheca Cantiana	(1837)
Toke, John,	Five Letters on the State of the Poor in the County of Kent. (published anonymously)	(1770)
Webb, Sidney and	The Parish and the County	(1906)
Beatrice,	English Poor Law History	(1929)
	The Story of the King's Highway	(1920)
Wye Local History	(the Journal of Wye Historical Society)	

Acts of Parliament

2 & 3 Philip and Mary, c.8	(1555)	(Highways)
43 Eliz. I, c.2	(1601)	(Poor Law)
I James I, c.37	(1603)	(Hares)
30 Chas. II, c.3	(1679)	(Burials)
3 & 4 William & Mary, c.12	(1691)	(Highways)
8 & 9 William III, c.30	(1697)	(Poor Law)
9 Geo. I, c.7	(1723)	(Poor Law "Knatchbull's Act")
17 Geo. II, c.5	(1744)	(Vagrancy)
26 Geo. II, c.30	(1753)	(Highways)
2 Geo. III, c.76	(1761)	(Faversham - Hythe Turnpike)
7 Geo. III, c.42	(1766)	(Highways)
2 Geo. III, c.83	(1782)	(Poor Law) ("Gilbert's Act")
35 Geo. III, c.101	(1795)	Poor Law
49 Geo. III, c.92	(1809)	(Stocker's Head to Chilham Turnpike)
4 & 5 William IV, c.77	(1834)	(Poor Law)
11 & 12 Victoria, c.63	(1848)	(Public Health)
25 & 26 Victoria, c.61	(1862)	(Highways)
57 & 58 Victoria, c.73	(1894)	(Local Government)

Wye Parish Records in Wye College Library

Churchwardens Accounts
1515-1663
1663-1692
1729-1766
1769-1789
1789-1819

Overseers Accounts (Poor Books)

1660-1691	1739-1753
1692-1704	1753-1764
1703-1724	1765-1788
1725-1739	1788-1804

Vestry Books
1724-1785   1785-1851

Highway Accounts
1827-1836

Certificate Book
1762

Index